"When Kevin Harney writes about reckless faith, I pay attention. Kevin is a great friend who seeks to live out his faith as a risk-taking, passionate, committed follower of Jesus. I highly recommend him—and his new book—to you!"

—**Lee Strobel**, *New York Times* bestselling author

"*Reckless Faith* is heartfelt, compelling, challenging, and convicting. As a pastor, I particularly appreciate Kevin Harney's wise guidance for living a faith that is responsibly focused on all-out surrender to the full counsel of God."

—**Gary Thomas**, writer in residence, Second Baptist Houston; author of *Sacred Marriage*

"Kevin and I have been peers in ministry for over twenty years. However, when I read *Reckless Faith*, he became the mentor and I the student."

—**Randy Frazee**, senior pastor, Oak Hills Church; author of *The Heart of the Story*

"If you think following Jesus takes the adventure out of life . . . think again! In *Reckless Faith*, Kevin reminds us that nothing could be further from the truth. Read it cover to cover to get in touch with the life God dreams for you to have."

—**Jim Mellado**, president, Willow Creek Association

RECKLESS FAITH

embracing a life

without limits

KEVIN G. HARNEY

BakerBooks

a division of Baker Publishing Group
Grand Rapids, Michigan

Published by Baker Books
a division of Baker Publishing Group
P.O. Box 6287, Grand Rapids, MI 49516-6287
www.bakerbooks.com

Printed in the United States of America

Library of Congress Cataloging-in-Publication Data
Harney, Kevin.
    Reckless faith : embracing a life without limits / Kevin G. Harney.
        p.   cm.
    Includes bibliographical references.
    ISBN 978-0-8010-1468-0 (cloth)
    1. Risk-taking (Psychology)—Religious aspects—Christianity. 2. Christian
life. 3. Martyrdom—Christianity. I. Title.
BV4598.15.H37 2012
248.4—dc23   2012023261

13   14   15   16   17   18   7   6   5   4   3

Through more than thirty years of following Jesus, I have been inspired by those who have lived for God with such reckless abandon that they paid the ultimate price for their faith—they lived and died for Jesus.

I dedicate this book to those heroes of the faith who have perished in prison, been torn to pieces by wild animals in arenas, held the hand of Jesus while burning at the stake, been killed by the very people they entered the mission field to reach with the gospel, and the countless multitude through history whose unyielding love for the Savior cost their very lives.

Tertullian said, "The blood of the martyrs is the seed of the church." May the passion of these brothers and sisters fill our hearts and drive us forward with reckless faith.

I dedicate this book to those who have gone before us and given an example of relentless pursuit of Jesus.

contents

acknowledgments

Special thanks to the wonderful publishing team at Baker. Your passion for *Reckless Faith* has inspired me in my writing of this book and the development of the video curriculum. Your striving for excellence assures me this book will be the best it can be. Finally, your desire to see Christians follow Jesus with reckless responsibility (and that is not an oxymoron) leads me to believe that this book will touch many lives for the glory of our one true God, Father, Son, and Holy Spirit.

—Kevin G. Harney

introduction

In the offbeat movie *A Mighty Wind*, there is a scene where one of the characters makes reference to a strange aspect of his upbringing. He is speaking of his mother and says, "She was very protective. You could say overly protective! I just like to think she cared for me. Which she did a lot. I was a member of the chess team. And whenever we had chess tournaments, I had to wear a protective helmet. I had to wear a football helmet. Now who knows what she was thinking? Maybe she thought we might have fallen and impaled our heads on a pointy bishop or something, I don't know." As he says these words, some old footage rolls and we see him as a young boy playing chess...while wearing an oversized football helmet.[1]

The scene is funny because it is absurd, ridiculous, over the edge.

Yet from the time I was a boy in the '60s and '70s, to the world today, our culture has become pathologically safety conscious. Kids now wear helmets while riding bikes, skiing, and maybe while playing board games if the safety police have their way. Warning stickers are on most children's toys, alerting parents to the imminent dangers present if their son or daughter swallows or chews on this item. In short . . . this toy could kill you! Children's car seats look like a device Houdini would have used in a magic show, complete with straps and buckles that take ten minutes to engage. The decks of community pools are covered with warnings: do not run, do not dive, do not jump, do not have fun!

Where will it end?

None of these safety concerns are bad, in and of themselves. They are simply a sign of the times. The world has not always been this obsessed with warning stickers, helmets, safety straps, and endless precautions.

I can vividly remember warm summer days as a young kid, growing up in Orange County, California. My mom would shout at me as I ran out the front door, "Be sure to come home when the streetlights come on." Often this would be six or seven hours later. We did not even have cell phones to function as an electronic tether to make sure our parents knew where we were at all times.

In the summer, during my junior high years, my mom would drop a bunch of us off at Huntington Beach in her blue station wagon as the sun was coming up in the morning. Someone else's mom would pick us up just before sunset, unless we were planning a bonfire—then we would stay even later.

We were risk takers, adventurers, and explorers forging our way through surrounding neighborhoods, eucalyptus groves, tomato fields, and the new housing developments of our rapidly emerging community. We rode bikes without helmets. We invented makeshift skateboards out of plywood in the garage and screwed spare wheels onto them. We rode these devices-of-death down hills, in empty pools, and spun in circles until we were dizzy. We used our dads' Skil saws as we created new kinds of skateboards . . . and we did not even wear protective eye gear!

The world was wild and ripe for adventure. It was a place of wonder and mystery to be discovered and devoured. It was glorious!

The world has changed.

We have been tamed and domesticated.

Adventure and intrigue happen less frequently in the real world. Now young people sit in the glow of a television or computer monitor as they navigate virtual worlds, with skillful thumbs and fingers guiding complex controllers of the newest gaming system.[2]

Deep in the soul of each new generation lies a longing for reckless adventure. Too often it is found in a digital format and not face-to-face with the flesh and blood of the real world. Reality television is birthing a generation of voyeurs who live vicariously through the fabricated stories of "real people" on a growing host of shows that reflect anything and everything except reality.

Into our increasingly safe, sedentary, and tame world comes the wild Aslan. He is C. S. Lewis's "Jesus figure," the Great Lion of Narnia who wants us to know that he is not tame or safe![3] Jesus speaks to a passive and sedentary world, offering to inject us with the adrenaline of his presence and take us on a reckless adventure of epic glory. God is ready to call us out of passivity and into a new season of life that is exciting, challenging, and worth living. God's vision is a life without layer after layer of precautions and limits.

Pause and reflect on each of these important questions:

Am I ready to accept God's invitation and take new risks?

Do I desire to live a life of faith that is truly reckless?

Do I long to take a journey of faith without limits or fear?

Will I follow Jesus on his adventure, no matter what the cost or where it leads?

Your answers to these questions will determine the trajectory of your life.

1

from domesticated to adventurous

I sat on the back deck of our home on a muggy summer day in Michigan. My youngest son, Nate, was stretched out like a cat in the sun, soaking in the heat of the afternoon. He had been jumping in and out of our above-ground pool to enjoy the feeling of the water evaporating off his skin. He was in junior high at the time.

As I looked at him, I saw his eyes wander from the pool up to the dormer window of his second-floor bedroom and then back to the pool again. After studying the slope of the roof and the distance down to the cool water of the pool, Nate said, "Dad, if I climbed out my bedroom window and ran across the roof, do you think I could jump and land in the middle of the pool?"

He was not really asking for permission . . . at this point. He was pondering the mathematics of the roof's slant, the distance he would have to run, and the actual drop to the water in the pool. He knew we had dug out a deep spot in the middle of the pool and this would be the bull's-eye for landing if he were to execute this daring feat with the greatest hope of success.

I joined him in studying the science of the situation. He and I both lay on the deck, looking up at the window, the pitch of the roof, and then at the water in the pool below.

I said, "I think you would need to climb out the window, hold the corner of the dormer for stability, get good footing, and actually run up the roof a bit, make an arc to the right, and then jump to the middle of the pool."

We both agreed that this would be the best plan of attack.

I went on to say, "I have been wondering how long it would take one of you boys to figure out this possibility."

I was telling the truth. I had often thought that I would have been launching myself off the roof and into the pool long before this, had I been the age of my three boys.

"Are you saying I can do it?"

I responded, "I think you should!"

We went on to discuss safety issues, possible consequences if he lost his footing, and the importance of my being near while this experiment transpired.[1] I explained that I did not think it would be all that dangerous because he was a coordinated kid and a great swimmer. I also told him that he should never do this unless I was present as a safety backup and lifeguard. We talked about how he might get injured if he lost his footing and fell on the deck or missed the pool when he jumped.

Nate spent the better part of the next hour jumping off the roof into the pool. It was quite exquisite. He mastered the arc across the roof and the launch into the pool, and ripped the landing (feet first, of course). After about an hour of successful flights into the pool, he grew bored with it and moved on to some other activity.

It turned out that the only real and present danger was his desire to run through the house and upstairs without fully drying off between jumps, thus leaving water all over the house.

When Nate's friends asked if they could join him, the answer was different. We let them know that their parents would have to sign a release waiver.

None of them joined in.

I could write a book of all the adventurous things my boys did through the years. They were raised to take risks, live on the edge, and be a bit reckless. They were also taught to be responsible and thoughtful when doing so.[2] I am convinced this is part of what has shaped the bold men they are today.

Recklessness Goes Deeper

One day when our roof-jumping son Nate was in high school, he asked Sherry and me, "Can we sit down and talk?" We gave each other a quick parental glance, both wondering what this could be about, and joined Nate at the dining room table.

He was very serious and sober. "You both know that I want to spend my life serving Jesus." His statement was a reminder, not a question.

Years before, Nate had expressed a sense of call to some kind of vocational ministry, either pastoral or missions work. He knew he would invest his life in serving God through full-time Christian service.

Nate went on. "I want you to know that I am ready to go anywhere God calls me. I am ready to do whatever God wants me to do."

Then he paused, looked directly at us, and said these words: "I am ready to die for Jesus if that is what he calls me to do!"

He looked at his mom, and so did I. God has given my wife, Sherry, amazing gifts of compassion and sensitivity. She is a tenderhearted person, and her point of greatest sensitivity centers on our three boys. I knew Nate's words would go deep into Sherry's mother-heart.

I instinctively reached under the table and placed my hand gently on her leg and gave a soft squeeze. No words were exchanged, but she knew what this gesture was saying— "Just listen. Receive what Nate is communicating. Don't be a tender mama, but let this young man express this deep sense of calling and reckless surrender to Jesus."

We sat for a moment and then Sherry spoke. "Nate, we love you and want you to live a life fully surrendered to God. You need to do whatever he calls you to do and go wherever he leads you. We will support you no matter what the cost." I echoed the same heartfelt commitment, we had a prayer together, and he headed out to see some friends.

Sherry and I sat there in silence for a few moments, pondering the reality that our son had just told us he was ready and willing to die for his faith in Jesus. I think we were both reflecting on where this kind of reckless willingness and surrender might lead our son.

After a few minutes Sherry went into our bedroom, closed the door, and shed a few tears . . . asking God to help her release Nate fully to his will and work. I gave her a little time to be alone and process her feelings. Later we prayed together and talked about the heart of a young man so surrendered to God that he was ready to go anywhere, do anything, and serve no matter what the cost. This reckless spirit of commitment and passion touched us both deeply.

Do you ever wonder if our heavenly Father is waiting for his children to take a few more risks for his sake? Is there a hunger in your soul for a fresh new adventure and an infusion of the exhilaration that comes when you seek first his kingdom and his righteousness?[3]

Irresponsible Recklessness?

I know, at this point some readers are wondering, is this guy going to write a whole book about jumping off roofs and taking crazy risks without stopping to consider the consequences? Is this an invitation to thoughtless and ir-responsible actions? If you are pondering this, the answer is a sincere "No!"

I am a huge proponent of reckless faith, but I also believe in what I call *responsible recklessness*. This means we don't just go out and do something because it is dangerous or risky. Instead, we are to walk through a very thoughtful process of discerning what risks God wants us to take and what will lead to his glory.

God calls us to take up the cross daily and follow Jesus.[4] This is a call to sacrifice everything. It is an invitation to come and die. Radical surrender and reckless faith are part of the journey of walking with the Savior.

Sadly, some people use the biblical call to radical disciple-ship and holy recklessness as an excuse for license or a cloak for irresponsibility. When I hear a story of a young person who decides to drop out of college and travel to Europe to work at a "Christian coffee house," with a plan to change the world through serving vanilla lattes, I have to wonder if this is a reckless leading of the Spirit or the longing of a kid who is tired of school. I have heard people explain that they are not working because they are writing a book that will "change the world," and they pawn off their reckless enterprise on God while their family spirals toward poverty, and I wonder . . . is this really a call from God? I have seen pastors live recklessly and work endlessly for Jesus as their marriage fell apart and their children grew bitter . . . all the time blaming God for their lack of boundaries and poor decisions. I am not saying God can't call someone to start a coffee house in Europe, spend many hours writing a book they are passionate about, or work tirelessly for Jesus, but we need to stop and ask if there is a difference between being personally irresponsible and being called to reckless faith by Jesus.

I worry that sometimes we act on personal impulse and label it "the call of God." I suspect there are times we jump off a cliff with reckless abandon and then ask God to bless us, when he would prefer we keep our feet firmly planted on the rock of Jesus. I have a gut feeling there are lots of times we want to brand something we do as reckless faith for the sake of God's kingdom when it is really irresponsibility on our part, and God does not want the credit or the blame.

I have watched men run off on a harebrained scheme or business enterprise, risking the security of their family and the future of their children, and they throw it all on God by saying, "I am taking a risk for the Lord." If it really is a risk for God, called by God, and inspired by the Holy Spirit . . . great! But if it is a personal dream that is ill-planned and destined for failure, blaming it on God (or trying to give God the credit) is irresponsible at best and deceptive at worst.

Reckless faith is a God-ordained leap of faithfulness inspired by the Holy Spirit and consistent with Scripture. Irresponsible recklessness is a personal pursuit of what I want, with little prayer, accountability, or wisdom. God celebrates reckless faith, but he wants us to avoid irresponsible recklessness.[5]

Responsible Recklessness Matrix

To help us grow in reckless faith and stay responsible along the way, there are three simple principles that can guide any person seeking to live a reckless life of faith, but also honor God as they seek to be responsible on the journey.

I suggest using this matrix—consisting of three filters—to help us determine if we are being people of reckless faith or just being irresponsible. Each of these filters begins with the letter *P* and will help create space for the Holy Spirit to speak and lead as we seek to live a life of God-honoring reckless faith.

1. Prayer

The first commitment is *prayer*. As you begin to take steps of reckless faith, pray deeply. Talk to God about it. Listen for his leading.

Jesus is clear that the sheep of his pasture hear his voice and follow him.[6] Before we run off on some reckless adventure or make a risky decision, we need to spend significant time in prayer one-on-one with God and praying in community with other Christians we respect. We should listen to the still small voice of the Holy Spirit.

If we will not take time to pray and listen for the Lord's leading, there is a good chance we are not operating in reckless faith but in personal irresponsibility!

2. Perspective

The second concept that will temper and guide a life of reckless faith is *perspective*. We can't see the whole picture. Our minds are not wise enough to understand all the implications of our decisions. Our eyes can't see as far down the road as we need to. We need to gain perspective that will shape and guide our decisions—particularly when we are living a life of reckless faith.

There are two essential sources for gaining perspective. The first and most important is the Bible, God's Word. If we are heading toward a course of action, taking a risk, and seeking to be reckless for the sake of God, we must look to the Word of God to gain direction and clarity. I have sat and talked with Christians who declared what they were about to do was for God. But the clear teaching of the Bible would call them to a very different course of action. In these moments, the loving thing to do is point out that God's Word stands in disagreement with their decision. In short, the Bible is right and their idea of reckless faith is wrong.

By testing our sense of what reckless faith should look like against the truth revealed in the Bible, we can get a fresh and new perspective. Since the Scriptures are inspired by God, they give us a look farther down the road than we can see on our own. This is a desperately needed perspective for people who want to live with reckless faith. The clear teaching of

Scripture always trumps our sense of adventure or feelings about what we should do. If God's Word affirms our sense of leading . . . great! If the Bible disagrees with what we want to do, then we align with the teaching of Scripture and submit to God's revealed truth.

Our second source of perspective will come from people who have godly wisdom and care about our future. When we feel a call to reckless faith and want to take a bold chance for Jesus, we are wise to draw together a few people who know us, our heart, our personal history, and who love God passionately. We should ask for their perspective and listen very closely to what they say. We are wise when we humbly invite the input, prayers, and outlook of mature Christians.[7]

This does not mean we must do what they say. It does not mean we are giving them permission, over the leading of God, to direct our future. What it does mean is that we invite their outlook and wisdom and let their unique perspective impact how we are looking at things and what we are planning to do. If we hear a refrain of warning or caution from various people who give us godly counsel, we are wise to pay attention. If we get consistent affirmation and encouragement to press on, we draw confidence from their wisdom to move forward.

All through the Scriptures God uses people to speak his message to other believers. He might just want to do that for you as you invite the perspective of other believers you love and trust.

3. Patience

Finally, if we want to live with responsible recklessness, we should grow a very specific fruit of the Holy Spirit . . . *patience*.[8] Once we have prayed and gained perspective from the Bible and wise people, we should take time, slow down, and be patient. Don't jump the moment some impulse hits you.

Suppose you hear a sermon on world missions and you are so inspired that you decide you are going to quit your job tomorrow, move to India, and share the gospel. You get points for passion and enthusiasm, but wisdom says, "Cool your jets! Pray. Get perspective. Be patient. Research the mission field. Talk with mission organizations. Assess your financial situation. Use your mind. Pray some more." If you get confirmation in prayer, and the perspective of trusted Christian friends is that this could be a call from God and you are uniquely qualified to do this, great! Remember, the needs and opportunity will still be there in a few months. Take your time and plan wisely. Often the most effective steps of reckless faith are taken slowly and over time.

Don't forget that God placed Moses in a desert to serve as a shepherd before he was prepared to lead the people of Israel out of Egypt.[9] Jesus was thirty before he began his public ministry—and he was God![10] Patience, along with prayer and perspective, will help you determine if you are on course for a grand adventure of reckless faith, or standing on the ledge of disaster.

In our tame and domesticated world, God is looking for risk takers, roof jumpers, and a generation of people who will give God their whole life . . . without limits. But he wants us to use wisdom and discernment along the way. Reckless faith and stupidity can look like twin brothers, but they are radically different. In the chapters ahead, we will learn what a journey of reckless faith can really look like.

At the end of each chapter you'll find resources to help you dive deeper into what you've just read and learned. These challenges can be incorporated into your devotional time, explored when you finish the chapter, or woven naturally into your week as you follow the daily reading program (see pp. 193–96). If you don't have the time to review and utilize these resources right now, make it a point to come back to them later. It will be well worth your while—and could inspire reflection, prayer, and actions that will lead to a reckless life of faith!

Diving into Recklessness

>> Praying Reckless Prayers

Spend time on your own, or with other Christians, and pray in some of the following directions:

- Lord Jesus, teach me to take risks and chances that are both reckless and wise.
- Holy Spirit, remove my fears and apprehension so that I can take chances that will honor you and will make my life of faith an adventure.
- God, give me the wisdom to pray deeply, gain perspective through your Word and from other believers, and be patient as I seek to live a life of reckless faith.
- Please protect me from rushing off on my own adventure and missing the journey of reckless faith that you have planned for me.

>> Taking Reckless Actions

Pray and identify one reckless action or activity you have a strong sense that God has been prompting you to take for some time. Walk through the simple matrix discussed in this chapter:

1. *Pray* for clarity and God's leading concerning this action or activity.
2. Gain *perspective* through studying the Bible (is this action or activity encouraged in Scripture and consistent with the Word of God?). And gain additional perspective by sharing your thoughts and intentions with some respected Christian friends.
3. *Patiently* plan your next steps to move into action. Take the time you need to prepare and then jump in!

If you get green lights on all three levels of this process, take the plunge. Live the adventure. Take a leap of faith into the fresh waters of God's adventure for your life.

≫ Thinking Reckless Thoughts

Reflect on some of these questions in the coming days:

- What are some ways I have become domesticated, tamed, and have lost the adventure and excitement of my Christian faith?
- Which of the three *P*s in the Responsible Recklessness Matrix do I tend to avoid or miss—prayer, perspective, patience?
- What might God do in and through my life if I am willing to follow him with greater passion, take more chances, and enter a life of reckless faith?

2

an invitation to reckless faith

We moved to Byron Center, Michigan, and I became
the pastor of a wonderful church. I knew God had
called me to this congregation. I was excited.

I was also a fish out of water. I was a stranger in a strange
land.

It was my first experience of small-town life. I did not
know the customs, the social norms and mores. I had grown
up in Orange County, California, where one city merged into
another without the formalities of city signs or a declaration of the population in the next municipality. There was
not a lot of civic pride or a distinct sense of being part of a
unique city. We just lived in Orange County and knew that
the pavement started at the beach and ended at the base
of the mountains thirty miles inland . . . Just the way God
intended it!

When I moved to Michigan, I was in a place where civic
pride mattered, people cared that they were from Byron Center, Dorr, or even Moline, population 314! I was in a place

where everyone knew everyone and they all seemed to be related to each other. To be honest, it was unsettling.

The problem was, I was not related to anyone. I had never lived in a small town and no one gave me a rule book to guide me through the joys and landmines of small-town life.

With my wife and three little kids, I would spend the next couple of years being baptized into this new culture. I would step on toes, make mistakes, and have to offer my fair share of apologies for crossing lines I did not even know existed.

I can still remember going to my first small-town parade. One of my boys asked, "Dad, can we go to the Byron Center Parade?"

I asked, "Why?"

He just stared at me.

I pressed. "Who will be there?"

"Everyone!" he said.

I dug a little deeper, getting ready to mount my defense for why we should not show up at this seemingly trivial cultural affair and waste a perfectly good afternoon.

"How do you know everyone will be there?"

"Because they will!"

How do you argue with logic like that? I took another tack. "What is in the parade? Are there floats? Is there something special happening? Is there a theme?"

You have to understand, I lived in Pasadena, California, for five years and had been to the Rose Parade many times while growing up. I had the privilege of watching one of the best and most famous parades in the world, and even the renowned Rose Parade had a hard time keeping my attention. What was the Byron Center Parade going to offer? Great marching bands? Rose-covered floats? Celebrities?

The answer to all of these questions was a definitive "No!"

As far as I could tell, the Byron Center Parade had nothing that should have drawn a crowd.

Mystery Solved!

If you are a parent, you already know that I went to the parade. The power of my three boys and their persistent begging was too great for me to resist. I packed up a couple of beach chairs and headed to the corner of 84th Street and Byron Center Avenue. I fully expected there to be a few dozen people sitting along the street curbs, dozing off, as a few pickup trucks drove by filled with youth sports teams.

I could not have been more wrong!

If you are from a small town, you know who was at the parade . . . everyone! I'm serious. It seemed like the entire population of Byron Center was drawn to this event like moths to a bright porch light. I looked up and down the two main streets in town and there were crowds three and four people deep. Families came with beach chairs and blankets to stake out their territory. I don't think anyone spent the night reserving their spot, but I was shocked by the sheer number of people lining the streets. It almost looked like someone had bussed in extra people from nearby towns.

There was a buzz in the air. The parade was about to start. I was still baffled. Why were all these people here?

I know, parents wanted to see their son in his football jersey sitting on the back of a flatbed, siblings were there to see a big sister on the homecoming court wave from the passenger's seat of a convertible, and I was there to see two of my boys ride by on their bikes that were decorated with colorful streamers. But I was still mystified by the level of excitement and the countless kids lining the street with bags in their hands. The pieces had not yet fallen into place.

Then . . . the parade started and it all made sense.

When the first truck filled with the girls' high school soccer team came by, I got it!

Every person on every truck and in every car was holding a bucket or large bag of . . . CANDY! That's right. The participants in the parade were throwing candy into the crowds

26

lining the street. It was Pavlovian to the core. Promise you will hurl candy at kids and they will line the streets and salivate as they wait.[1]

For the next thirty minutes I studied this phenomenon. The crowds, the candy, and the whole thing fascinated me. As the parade passed by, I noticed that there were two distinct kinds of candy-throwing kids. In each truck and on each flatbed there were kids who were very reserved in their candy distribution. I watched as a boy looked into his candy bag and examined his hoard of sweets. He deliberated over which single piece he should throw. He would stare into the bag and, finally, carefully, place his hand in and draw out just the right piece.

Then, he would look at the crowd of kids as they stretched out their hands and screamed for candy. "Throw it, throw it here!" He would study each face, looking for just the right person (usually it seemed like he was looking for someone he knew). He would make eye contact and nod his head as if to say, "Are you ready?" He would wait for just the right moment to throw his one piece of candy. Sometimes, by the time he decided who should receive his snack-size Snickers bar, airmailed from the back of his moving perch, he was past that part of the route and he would begin looking for another possible recipient of his singular sugar treat.

It seemed like every float and truck had some kids like this. There were boys and girls who were so deliberate that they would go a long way down the parade route and never throw a single piece of candy into the frenzied crowd. I got the sense that some of them would finish the parade and still have a bucket full of candy. I found myself wondering if they thought they were going to get to keep whatever was left after the parade was done.

In dramatic contrast were the boys and girls who began down the parade route and would immediately start heaving candy at the crowds with two-fisted fury. These kids drove their little hands deep into the bag of candy on their lap, grabbed as much as they could, and let it fly! They took clear delight in watching the crowds on the sides of the street jump up to receive the airborne treats. They could not help themselves. They were candy-throwing machines. They were reckless!

I found myself thinking, *These kids will be out of candy about fifty yards down the parade route.* They were indiscriminate, passionate, lavish, and reckless in their candy-delivery duties.

As strange as it may sound, this experience at my first small-town parade (and subsequent experiences over the coming decade . . . we went to a lot of parades) made a significant impact on my faith. The unfettered and passionate recklessness of some of these kids painted a spiritual picture in my soul that I will never forget.

I found myself reflecting on my own life. Am I the safe kid in the back of the truck holding the vast riches of God's kingdom and tentatively doling out one piece at a time . . . when the moment seems perfect? Or am I the kid who grabs two handfuls of God's goodness, grace, and gospel and throws it out with reckless abandon?

I know what kind of kid I want to be! I am certain about the kind of person God wants me to be. I am praying, every day, that I will become a person who lavishly and recklessly shares the love and grace of God freely . . . everywhere I go.

What about you?

A Biblical Story of Reckless Extravagance

As long as I have been a Christian and reading the Bible I have loved the parable of the sower. It is an amazing story. Here is the text. Even if you have read it many times, please take a moment to read it again.[2] As you do, ask yourself this question: *Is there anything strange that jumps out at me in this story?*

While a large crowd was gathering and people were coming to Jesus from town after town, he told this parable: "A farmer went out to sow his seed. As he was scattering the seed, some fell along the path; it was trampled on, and the birds of the air ate it up. Some fell on rock, and when it came up, the plants withered because they had no moisture. Other seed fell among thorns, which grew up with it and choked the plants. Still other seed fell on good soil. It came up and yielded a crop, a hundred times more than was sown." When he said this, he called out, "He who has ears to hear, let him hear." . . .

"This is the meaning of the parable: The seed is the word of God. Those along the path are the ones who hear, and then the devil comes and takes away the word from their hearts, so that they may not believe and be saved. Those on the rock are the ones who receive the word with joy when they hear it, but they have no root. They believe for a while, but in the time of testing they fall away. The seed that fell among thorns stands for those who hear, but as they go on their way they are choked by life's worries, riches and pleasures, and they do not mature. But the seed on good soil stands for those with a noble and good heart, who hear the word, retain it, and by persevering produce a crop. (Luke 8:4–8, 11–15)

For years it never struck me. I never saw the behavior of this farmer as completely bizarre and over the edge. I grew up in an area where farming was on the way out and houses were being built as fast as possible. It was the end of the baby boom, and Orange County was exploding.

So, the local farmers were selling their land to developers and I never had a chance to observe how farming was done.

Had I grown up around farmers—more particularly, around poor farmers—I would have noticed the ridiculously reckless behavior of the sower in Jesus's story.

As it was, I had missed it.

Through the years, I have traveled to parts of the world where people are both poor and make their living through farming produce. Have you? If so, you will already know what I am getting at. People who live day-to-day, subsistence farming (like most did in the days of Jesus), would have treated seed with great care and caution. Seed was precious and expensive.

They would have plowed rows or furrows in which to plant their seed. They would have then moved along very carefully, painstakingly, and dug a single hole in the ground. Using their hands or a stick, they would have made this hole in the best soil they could find. Then they would have reached into a seed bag and taken out a single seed and carefully, sometimes prayerfully, planted it. With their own hands they would have covered the seed with good earth.

They would do this again, and again, and again, and again.

Every seed was precious. Each one mattered. Every seed had within it the hope of harvest, food, and life. No one would have recklessly thrown seed with no concern for where it would land.

Today I live just a few minutes from the Salinas Valley near the central California Coast. It is one of the most lush and fertile farm areas in the world. As a pastor in this region, I have many people in my church who work in the farming industry. I have asked some of them about the practices of farming and have learned that farmers have become even more attentive to how they use their seed. Larger farms use machines to plant the seed. These massive goliaths plant with precision and care. Every effort is taken to make sure no seed is wasted and every one can produce a harvest.

What was true for farmers in the days of Jesus is still true today. Seed is valuable, often expensive, and it is *not* to be wasted. A good farmer does not throw seed recklessly on hard-packed trails and into beds of weeds with no apparent concern for where it lands. No sane farmer in Jesus's day or our day would treat seed this way.

But this is not the picture we get when we watch the sower in Jesus's parable. He is *not* careful. He is *not* meticulous. He is *not* cautious. He is radically and irresponsibly reckless. This guy just throws seed . . . everywhere!

Rocky soil . . . throw some seed!
Weedy soil . . . blast it with seed!
Shallow soil . . . more seed flies!
That looks like good soil . . . seed, seed, seed!

Has this farmer lost his mind? Is he out of control, in need
of a week off on the Sea of Galilee for a little R&R so he can
pull himself together?

Get the Picture

Jesus is painting a picture that is vivid, vibrant, and coun-
tercultural—one that anyone in his day would have found
shocking. He is telling us about a reckless sower who seems
intent upon sowing and throwing seed everywhere he goes.

It is as if this farmer does not know if the soil is good or bad,
so he throws seed anyway . . . just in case the soil is receptive.

This sower reminds me of the boys and girls in the back
of the trucks going down the parade route in small-town
Byron Center who threw candy with extravagant generosity.

I have preached this parable many times over the years.
Often I have focused on the kinds of soil. It is a powerful
picture of different hearts, real people, who are open or closed
to the gospel. Those were good sermons and I believe they
were true to one message of the parable.

In recent years I have focused more on the sower. The reckless, irresponsible, out-of-control farmer who was throwing
seed on paths, in the weeds, in shallow and deep soil . . . everywhere! This sower is beautiful, bold, fearless, and reckless.

We Are Not Smart Enough to Know

Why in the world does Jesus tell this parable? I hope the answer is becoming obvious. He wants his followers, you and
me, to throw the seed of his love, grace, and gospel freely . . .

everywhere we go. He wants us to live with reckless faith. He longs for us to experience life without all the limits this world seeks to put on us.

We are called to scatter seed everywhere and all the time because—and I don't mean to offend—we are simply not smart enough to know the condition of the soil. I can't look at a person and know if their heart is like a hard path, weedy soil, or fertile ground that is truly receptive. I am just called to throw seed . . . recklessly, joyfully, and freely!

I thank God that the people who first shared the love and message of Jesus with me did not look at my long hair, apathetic attitude, or family history and make a decision that I was most likely not ready to respond to God's message of grace. They just threw seed. They loved me. They were generous. They served me like no one had ever served me before. They befriended me. They prayed for me. And they talked to me about this Jesus they all seemed to know so well.

They scattered seed, not knowing if it would land on receptive and soft soil or on a rock-hard heart. They salted my soul with grace, peppered my life with love, and emptied bag after bag of heavenly truth into my heart.

To a casual observer, there was nothing in my appearance or attitude that would have indicated that the soil of my heart was ready to embrace Jesus's love and grace. But they threw seed nonetheless. And by the amazing grace of God, I was ready. My heart opened and the seed of the gospel took root. Their reckless faith became the instrument God used to bring this wandering child to a place of repentance from sin and to friendship with Jesus.

For their recklessness, I am eternally grateful.

A Safety Net for Reckless Sowers

We live in a world where people worry too much and are anxious far too often. We can be like that kid in the parade who sits with our bag of candy and spends far too much time trying to determine if this is the right time to throw a piece. Is this the right kind of candy? Who should I throw it to? Are the wind conditions just right? Will someone catch the candy? The questions can be endless!

Here is the beauty of God's grace. When we are aggressively generous with the things of God, the bag never runs out. This is the safety net for reckless sowers. A kid on a parade route could run out of mini-Butterfingers and packs of Smarties, but we can't run out of God's grace. The more love we extend to others, the more we have. Jesus is calling us to be recklessly generous with his good news because there is more than enough to go around. We can throw it on the path, on the weedy ground, in the rocks, and on good soil, and we will still have a bag full of seed!

Where do we scatter God's love? Everywhere!

When do we dispense the amazing grace of Jesus? Always!

What if we run out of seed? We never will!

How can we know what a faith-filled life of recklessness looks like?

We look to Jesus, the trailblazer of recklessness.

Jesus, Trailblazer of Recklessness!

Michael and Gabriel approached Jesus, looking intently into his glorious face. As messengers of the living God, they drew near the Lord in the radiant glow of all their angelic beauty. In comparison to the blazing glory of the only Son of God, they seemed almost pale. On earth their power and beauty were startling. In the presence of other angels they were quite impressive. Compared to Jesus, they seemed almost ordinary.

"Is it true what we hear? Are you going down there and becoming one of them? Are you really going to become a man?"

A rumor had been floating around heaven. The Lord of Glory was planning to set aside his majestic beauty, empty himself, take on flesh, and enter human history.

Jesus looked at these two faithful warrior-servants and said, "No, I am not going there as a man."

Gabriel and Michael, at the same moment, let out angelic sighs of relief.

Then Jesus continued, "Not as a man, but as a baby."

The two angels stood before the Lord of Glory dumbfounded.

Gabriel spoke what both were thinking. "A baby? A crying, helpless, defenseless human baby?"

Jesus gazed at these two faithful messengers who had fought demons, stayed faithful to Yahweh, and served him so passionately. The Savior smiled. "Yes, a baby boy . . . with all that it means to be human . . . everything except sin!"

"But if you are a baby, if you grow up to be a boy and then a man . . . then you will be vulnerable!"

Michael blurted out, "They could kill you!"

Jesus looked back with bold confidence. "Only if I let them."

Of course this is just what I imagine could have transpired as Jesus got ready to enter human history, to come, to love, to die, to give his life for us. But you get the point. The greatest example of recklessness in the entire universe is found in Jesus. There is no more powerful example of reckless love, generosity, service, relationships, prayers, or words than the Savior himself.

As we accept the invitation to reckless faith, we follow in his steps. Jesus set the example. We seek to follow him, every day of our lives.

Diving into Reckless Faith

>> **Praying Reckless Prayers**

Spend time on your own, or with other Christians, and pray in some of the following directions:

- Ask God to help you become reckless in how you share his love, grace, and good news.
- Confess times when you have been like the kid who clings to his bag of candy and is resistant to just throw it out there.
- Thank God for the people he placed in your life who shared his love and care freely with you, even when you were not receptive or open.
- Lift up praise to Jesus for his reckless and extravagant love that led him to leave the glory of heaven and come to this world to bring you salvation and hope.

>> **Taking Reckless Actions**

Identify one person whom you have avoided or written off (when it comes to sharing the love and message of Jesus). You have seen this person as closed-hearted. In your mind, they are the hard, shallow, or weedy soil, and you have decided they are not ready to hear much about Jesus. Do three things in the coming days:

1. Begin praying for their heart to be open and receptive to God's seeking love.
2. Start praying for boldness in your heart and willingness to scatter some seed in their life.
3. Ask God what action of love, service, care, or what words of truth you can share with them.

Take any action God places on your heart. Also, keep praying for this person as you walk through this book. Ask God how you might exercise reckless faith as you engage in this relationship.

>> Thinking Reckless Thoughts

Reflect on some of these questions in the coming days:

- Who do I look like on most days—the kid who is resistant to throw candy or the one who smiles and chucks it out there with two hands?
- What can I do this week to become more generous in how I share the love, grace, and message of Jesus?
- Are there people in my life whom I have seen as "not ready or open to Jesus"? What if they just look like hard or weedy soil, but they are really open and ready to know Jesus?
- Who are the people in my life, right now, who need to know the truth and love of God? How might God use me to freely lavish their life with his love?

3

reckless love

It was my wife's thirty-fourth birthday and before I woke up, she had already received one of the best gifts of her life. It came from our middle son, Joshua. He was only five years old.

Instead of me trying to describe the story for you, I have asked Sherry to write an account of what happened that morning almost two decades ago:

> The day started like any other. By the end of the day I would look back and realize I had received one of the greatest gifts of my life. I received a little blue box that opened my eyes to the power and beauty of reckless love.
>
> It was early in the morning, before others were awake in our home. I was having some quiet time with God on the couch in the living room. I heard a stirring and looked up to see my son quietly trying to sneak past me. Josh, our then five-year-old, was headed to our bedroom. I found it curious that he was up this early and wondered if he had remembered it was my birthday. I listened, trying to figure out what he might be up to.

I realized he had snuck into my closet. I knew there was a box filled with cards for all occasions tucked in the corner, but did not know if Josh was aware of this. I was surprised when Josh appeared several minutes later with a card in one hand and a little unwrapped blue box in the other. It wasn't just any box—it was his favorite school box.

He walked over to the couch where I was reading and quietly handed me the card and box as he said, "Happy birthday, Mom." I was amazed and deeply touched by this kind act of my little boy—and this, so early in the morning! Even if there had been nothing in the box, the very thoughtfulness of his actions had already brought joy to my mother's heart.

I looked at his little face and said, "Oh Josh, thank you so much."

As I opened the card, which I still have, I had to smile. Instead of addressing it to MOM, he had written it to say WOW. He was still working on getting his Ws and Ms figured out, and it was quite early in the morning. He signed the card, "Love You." There were all sorts of cards in that box in my closet and I was pleased that he had actually found a birthday card and not pulled out a sympathy card.

As I thanked Josh, he just smiled. I held the little gift box on my lap. It was covered with pictures of racing cars and classic cars. Josh sat quietly as I opened the gift box and looked at the contents. To my surprise there were four items in this special school box. As I looked at them, I realized that each item reflected Josh's love for me.

I took each little gift out of the box and held it in my hand. I was overwhelmed by a deep sense that this was a special moment of love between a mother and her son. The first item was his favorite little Matchbox car. I turned to Josh, thanking him for such a sacrificial gift. I told him that I knew this was his favorite car. He just nodded.

The second gift was a quarter. I realized this was all the money he had accessible to him at the time. "Josh, how special that you would give me all the money in your room."

The third gift was a handheld toy that he always took with him whenever we traveled in our car. It was a little pinball game. This was before video games, cell phones, or electronic gadgets were used to entertain kids while traveling. He loved this little toy.

I sat there and thought to myself, *Wow, could this gift get any better! His favorite school box, all the money he had to give, his favorite Matchbox car, and his special travel toy.* You can imagine the heart of a mother receiving such a loving and sacrificial gift.

As I looked back in the box to retrieve my last item, the significance of this gift was not as obvious to me. I picked up the item and held it in the air so both Josh and I could see it.

It was a set of play handcuffs.

I knew there had to be significance to this gift but was unable to come up with it as I had with the previous three. I was a second-grade schoolteacher, so I used my teaching skills to unravel this mystery. Kindly, I asked him, "Josh, what were you thinking of when you put this in my special gift box?"

He said quietly, "Well, I was thinking since today is your birthday, maybe you could put one handcuff on your arm, and I could put the other one on my arm, and we could spend the whole day together."

Tears welled up in my eyes. "Oh Josh, thank you so much, I would love to spend the day with you." And we did!

That experience has become a picture of reckless love that I continue to remember and share with others. In that moment, the Holy Spirit impressed this thought on me: "You know the joy you feel right now toward your son? That's how I feel when you want to be with me." I knew God was teaching me through Josh's gift box. I was overjoyed that my son would give with such sacrifice. I was also touched that what he wanted most was just to be with me.

When I woke up that morning and Sherry told me the story and showed me the little gift box, we both had a sense that this was a sacred moment. Since then we have talked often about wanting to love God with that kind of passion and recklessness. We want to give him everything we have in the box of our life, and top it off by saying, "And what I want most is to be handcuffed to you all day long!"

I think God would like that.

The Pinnacle of Recklessness

Of all the reckless things we should do, love is on the top of the list. It always has been. It always will be! Jesus was emphatic about this:

> One of the teachers of the law came and heard them debating. Noticing that Jesus had given them a good answer, he asked him, "Of all the commandments, which is the most important?"
>
> "The most important one," answered Jesus, "is this: 'Hear, O Israel, the Lord our God, the Lord is one. Love the Lord your God with all your heart and with all your soul and with all your mind and with all your strength.' The second is this: 'Love your neighbor as yourself.' There is no commandment greater than these." (Mark 12:28–31)

There it is! Simple, crystal clear, and right from the very lips of Jesus.

Love God.
Love people.

This is the very center, bull's-eye, and heart of the Christian life. If we want to live with reckless faith, love will be the fuel that drives everything else.

We should not run out and engage in a laundry list of "Good Christian" activities, thinking this is the full substance of love. Instead we begin by letting our hearts be captured and enraptured by the love of God. The starting point of reckless faith is not our good works or religious activity. It is a profound and deep awareness that we are loved beyond our wildest imagination.

I Want a *Real* Friend

When I first became a follower of Jesus, I discovered that a number of my closest friends did not want to hang out with me any longer. I did not leave these friendships or walk away from these people. I cared about them and wanted them to know the love of Jesus I was discovering. I still wanted to be their friend. But some of them shut the relational door on me because I would no longer engage in the same behaviors and activities that were part of our past.

I was working at building new friendships with Christians, but this took time. For a couple of months I was very lonely. My two best friends would have nothing to do with me because I had become a Christian.

I remember sitting on the edge of my bed one morning and praying, "God, please help me build some new friendships with other Christians. Let my old friends not block me out of their lives." As I talked with God, I heard him speak to me, gently in my heart, one simple line: "I will be your closest friend."

I reflected on this amazing offer extended by the God of the universe and responded to him with these words: "But I want a real friend."

I have to believe my heavenly Father had a warmhearted chuckle in response to my childlike request. The Lord of eternity offered to be my best friend and I suggested that I wanted a legitimate friendship.

What I have learned through the years is that God is my closest and best friend. He loves me and I love him! With each passing day, this friendship grows, deepens, and becomes even more powerful. If we want to discover the joy of reckless faith, a close and loving relationship with God is foundational.

It Begins with God . . . Always!

The God who spoke the heavens into existence, and who sustains the universe by his word of power, loves you and me. He really does! His affection and care for us started long before we repented of our sins or cried out for the grace revealed in

Jesus. The apostle Paul penned some of the most joyful and sobering words in the history of humanity when the Holy Spirit led him to write,

> You see, at just the right time, when we were still powerless, Christ died for the ungodly. Very rarely will anyone die for a righteous man, though for a good man someone might possibly dare to die. But God demonstrates his own love for us in this: While we were still sinners, Christ died for us. (Rom. 5:6–8)

God expressed his love by sending his only Son to die on the cross, in our place, for our sins. He did this while we were still hate-filled, rebellious, and sinful people.

Is the picture growing clearer? Love does not begin with our confession of sin, as important as this is. It does not originate with our initiative and surrender to God. Love does not start when we decide to open our hearts, arms, and lives to Jesus.

He initiated love.

God got the ball rolling.

His love launched the plan for restoration and salvation, and we are the recipients of undeserved and unearned grace. In the book of Ephesians, we read, "For it is by grace you have been saved, through faith—and this not from yourselves, it is the gift of God—not by works, so that no one can boast."[1] Jesus pointed to this reality when he walked on this earth and declared, "Greater love has no one than this, that he lay down his life for his friends."[2]

We live on the other side of the cross and the empty tomb, so we know the rest of the story. Jesus proved the depth and purity of his love when he willingly offered his life on the cross as the payment for our sins. If all of this does not paint the picture with vivid clarity, the apostle John writes these words that capture the heart of every person who has received the amazing grace of Jesus: "This is love: not that we loved God, but that he loved us and sent his Son as an atoning sacrifice for our sins."[3] Love is not, first and foremost, about what we do, think, or feel. It is about God's reckless sacrifice and entry into this broken world. It is about an old rugged cross on Calvary's hill. It is about the broken body and poured-out blood of the sinless and holy Son of God.

Love begins at the cross. If it does not, it is a counterfeit.

Love comes to us when we encounter the God who so loved the world that he gave his only Son.[4] Love begins to flow within us as we look into the sweat-covered, bloodstained, tear-streaked, brutalized face of the crucified Savior who completed the work of redemption on our behalf and cried out, "IT IS FINISHED!"[5] Love begins to flow through us when we are filled with the Holy Spirit of God and allow his love to become our own.[6]

When we are captured by his love and transfixed by his beauty, his amazing grace will change the world through his sons and daughters. This is the beginning of reckless love.

How to Love God First . . . Before All of the "These" in Our Lives

We must love God first and above all else. If we want to be equipped to love other believers and to bring God's love to our hurting and broken world, we must love him with a reckless passion that surpasses all other devotion. That is why Jesus was emphatic that we love God with everything in us. This is the first and greatest commandment.[7] When we learn to love God, we can take the second step and love our neighbors.[8]

If we are going to love God first, we will have to identify the things that get in the way and compete for first place in our hearts. Naming these potential idols and casting them down is a part of loving God.

All four of the Gospels record the account of Peter, one of Jesus's closest friends, denying the Savior three times.[9] Peter was public with his rejection of the Lord and forceful as he swore he did not know Jesus. He even invoked a curse on himself if he knew who Jesus was.[10] After his denial, Peter wept bitterly. He was broken and confused.

Jesus was crucified, dead, and buried.

Peter went back to his old job—he went fishing.

There is an encounter reported only in the fourth Gospel where the risen Lord meets with Peter face-to-face and talks about the topic of love.[11] You might have heard a sermon or two about the way Jesus asked Peter, "Do you love me?" three times. It is a powerful picture of Peter having a chance to publicly and repeatedly affirm that he still loved the Lord. Each time Peter expressed his love, Jesus gave him a ministry task.

There is a good chance Peter felt disqualified and unworthy to do the kind of ministry he had been engaged in for the past three years. This was the Lord's way of letting Peter know that he could still be used to serve God and minister to people. After this conversation with Jesus, Peter knew his future would not be about pulling in nets full of fish from the Sea of Galilee. He would once again be used by God to fish for men and women.[12]

There is one little part of this story of Peter's post-resurrection encounter with Jesus that does not get discussed very often. One word in verse 15 of John 21 has several possible meanings—the word "these." Jesus asks Peter, "Simon, son of John, do you truly love me more than these?" Here is the question: What is Jesus talking about when he says "these"?

Here are four possible ways to understand the word "these" in this passage:

1. Peter, do you love me more than you love *these* fish you just hauled in?
2. Peter, do you love me more than you love *these* boats and nets?
3. Peter, do you love me more than you love *these* disciples?
4. Peter, do you love me more than *these* other disciples love me?

Which is the right way to read "these" in the passage? I would suggest we could learn from all four options. Maybe the word is vague because each one has something to teach us about reckless love for God and devotion to him above all else.

Do You Love Me More than Material Wealth and Success?

Jesus could have been asking Peter, "Do you love me *more than these fish*?" This might seem like a strange question to us, but we have to realize that Peter grew up as a fisherman and a son of a fisherman. This was the family business. When Jesus called Peter to follow him, he asked him to leave fishing to enter a life of ministry. Peter had sat at the family dinner table countless evenings hearing his dad talk about the day's catch.

"We brought in thirty-seven fish today!"

"There was not a fish in the lake today. We cast the nets over and over and over and not one fish to show for it."

"It was an amazing day, eighty-seven fish, and they were huge! You should have seen the one that got away!" The stories would have gone on into the evening. If you fish, you understand that fishing is the first part of the day and the stories are part two.

Peter and his buddies had just come in from an epic day of fishing. For three years Peter had left the business and spent his days fishing for people, sharing the love of God. Now he had denied Jesus, his friend had died on a cross, and Peter had gone back to his old job. The day recorded in this story was not just another day of fishing. Peter and his friends had just caught the mother lode! Someone actually counted and there were 153 fish. The passage is very specific . . . they were *large* fish. This was the kind of haul that would normally tear a net apart, but the nets were fine. It was an extraordinary day of fishing!

What if Jesus was asking Peter, "Do you love me more than this huge pile of fish?" If this was the case, he would have been saying, do you love me more than wealth and success? When Peter looked at a net full of fish, he could do the math without even thinking. He knew what fish were worth in the market. Like a prospector hitting gold, Peter knew the rush and excitement of a big haul coming in. This was payday!

Here's the question for you and me: Do you love Jesus more than a big pile of fish, or a great day on the stock market, or your weekly paycheck, or your net worth, or your savings account, or . . . you get the point. Reckless love for God declares, "I love you more than the stuff of this world that sparkles, shines, and seems so important." The Bible never says money is bad, but loving money leads to all kinds of evil.[13] As we seek to grow recklessly in love with God, he must always come before our pursuit of material things. As hard as it is to understand, seeking him first is the key to living a balanced and reckless life of love. Jesus put it this way:

> So do not worry, saying, "What shall we eat?" or "What shall we drink?" or "What shall we wear?" For the pagans run after all these things, and your heavenly Father knows that you need them. But seek first his kingdom and his righteousness, and all these things will be given to you as well. Therefore do not worry about tomorrow, for tomorrow will worry about itself. Each day has enough trouble of its own. (Matt. 6:31–34)

Do You Love Me More than Security?

Jesus could have been asking Peter, "Do you love me *more than these boats and nets?*" This would have been a way of saying, "Peter, what do you love more, me or security?" You see, Jesus was about to leave the earth. In a very short time the risen Savior would ascend to heaven in glory. Before Jesus would be taken up, he would call Peter to follow him away from the fishing business and back to a life of preaching and ministry. Jesus is about to call Peter away from security and into a journey of faith.

Peter and the disciples would be without the friend who had led them for the past three years. In Peter's world, boats and nets were security. If you had a boat and net, you could eat. You could provide for your family. "Peter, what do you love more, me or the family business?"

What is your boat and net? What makes you secure? Are you ever tempted to make personal security more important than God? If you do, then security has become an idol. This is not to say that a good job, a savings account, or planning for the future is wrong. These things can all be very good. But if we love security more than God, and if boats and nets become more important than Jesus, we will have a hard time living with reckless love. We must love God first if we want to experience the best and fullest life of faith.

Do You Love Me More than You Love Anyone Else?

Perhaps Jesus was asking Peter, "Do you love me *more than you love these other disciples?*" Again, this could seem like a strange question, but remember, Peter had just denied Jesus three times in a very public setting. When we burn a bridge with one friend, it is not unusual to work harder at strengthening the ties of friendship with someone else. Maybe Jesus wanted Peter to be clear that no other human relationship should take supremacy over his relationship with Jesus. This would not have been inconsistent with other things Jesus had said:

> Large crowds were traveling with Jesus, and turning to them he said: "If anyone comes to me and does not hate his father and mother, his wife and children, his brothers and sisters— yes, even his own life—he cannot be my disciple. And anyone who does not carry his cross and follow me cannot be my disciple." (Luke 14:25–27)

Of course Jesus is not advocating hatred of family. He is speaking in hyperbole to make a point.[14] What he is saying is, "Your devotion to me should be absolutely passionate, deep, and recklessly loving. In comparison to your love for me, all other relationships could seem like hatred."

Is it possible for us to let human relationships become the focus of our life? Can we stumble into letting a spouse, a boyfriend or girlfriend, a colleague at work, a child, or some other person become more important than Jesus? If we do, we risk the joys and benefits of reckless love.

The truth is, we can't love others well if we do not love God first. I experience this in my life on a regular basis. If I am loving God recklessly and staying closely connected with Jesus, I love my wife better, I care for my sons with greater strength, I serve my staff members with more tenderness, and I notice the needs of neighbors and am more willing to help them. When I get things backward and don't make time to stay deeply connected to the Savior, the people who know me well can see it. As a matter of fact, I rarely have to say anything . . . it starts to show. My wife will come to me and gently ask, "Are you spending time with God? How is your walk with Jesus?" She can see the change in me before I notice it in myself.

You can probably guess how I respond to my wife when she asks me if I am walking closely with Jesus (and am not). In these moments I am usually brusque, defensive, and sometimes a bit hostile. My negative response simply affirms that my life is out of balance and Sherry's suspicions are correct.

If we desire to love others well, we will make sure we love God first. The best gift a husband or wife can give their spouse is to develop a reckless love relationship with God. Any parent who wants to love their family well will be sure to love God first and deeply. This holds true for every relationship in our life. Never let love for any person supplant your commitment to loving God first.

Do You Love Me with a Humble Heart?

The final option for what Jesus could have meant by "these" might seem the strangest of all. It could be that he was asking Peter, "Do you love me *more than these other disciples love me?*"

What an odd question this would have been. Why in the world would Jesus force Peter to declare, out loud, that he loved him more than anyone else? Remember, some of the other disciples were sitting right there.

To understand this, we need to go back to the table at the Last Supper just a few days earlier. Jesus was gathered with his followers, and he announced that they were all going to fall away. Peter was the first to respond to these hard words, and he made this bold and confident statement: "Even if all fall away on account of you, I never will."[15]

Just chew on those words for a minute.

Peter was sitting with the other disciples and he declared, "They might all fall away, but when the dust settles, you can know that I will be by your side!" You can almost hear Peter: "Jesus, I'm the rock! Remember, you gave me that nickname. This is Peter you're talking to. How could you think that I would ever deny you?"

Jesus then responds to Peter's declaration of absolute certainty in himself and tells him, "Peter, the truth is, you will deny me three times before the morning comes."[16] Peter's response is stronger than his first declaration. He tells Jesus, "Even if I have to die with you, I will never disown you."[17]

Now turn the clock ahead a few days. Peter has denied Jesus three times, just as the Lord said. Jesus has died on the cross. Peter has gone back to fishing. And now Peter and Jesus are face-to-face. They are gathered with a group of disciples, having a meal again, and Jesus asks, "Simon, son of John, do you truly love me more than these?" He just might be asking, "Peter, do you still think you love me more than anyone else does?"

If this is what Jesus is asking, it is interesting to note that Peter does not say, "Yes, Lord, you know I love you more than *these*." What he says is, "Yes, Lord, you know that I love you."[18] There is no comparison in his response.

Jesus could be teaching Peter the importance of loving him with a humble heart. Our Savior does not want his followers comparing themselves with others, but simply loving out of who we are. We are to love God with all our heart, soul, mind, and strength.[19] We are not called to love God more than other people do, but just to love him as recklessly and fully as we can.

As we seek to love God well, we need to make a commitment to never play the comparison game. "At least I love God more than she does!" "Well, compared to that guy, I really love God." "In our church we really know how to love God, how to worship, how to pray, how to serve . . . [ad infinitum . . . ad nauseam]".[20] God's heart breaks when we play these childish games. We are called to love him with everything we have, with reckless love. He is not comparing our love to others and neither should we.

So, what's the right answer?

Which of these four options is the exact and correct way to understand the word "these" in this passage? I believe all four options are exactly that—options. Maybe that's why Jesus used the word "these" and was not more specific. If we read the Bible closely, we discover that God does call us to love him more than riches (we will look at that in the next chapter), more than security, and even more than we love the other people in our lives. God calls us to love him first and fully. When we do this, we are filled and ready to extend God's love to others. When we love God and seek his kingdom first, the rest of the pieces of our lives will fall into place.[21]

A Picture of Reckless Love

I have a friend who is a pastor and church leader in Sri Lanka. His name is Ajith Fernando. I love this man for many reasons. He is passionate and uncompromising about the gospel, he is devoted to prayer, he loves his family, and he serves the church tirelessly. In addition to this, he is a wonderful theologian and has written some of my favorite books.[22] Perhaps one of the things that has most struck me about this man is his reckless love for Jesus.

On one of Ajith's trips to the United States, he came and spoke at the church I was serving and stayed for a few days in our home. We had a number of conversations, and I found myself learning so much from this humble and godly man. At one point I asked, "Ajith, do you ever think about moving to another part of the world to serve and minister?" We had been discussing the civil unrest in Sri Lanka and the ongoing persecution of Christians that happens in that part of the world on a fairly regular basis.

He smiled at me and said, "I do get a lot of offers, and many people ask me if I think of living somewhere safer. But I will live and die among my people. That is where God has called me." He spoke with gentle confidence. I knew what he was saying. He was not simply declaring, "I will die of old age in Sri Lanka." Ajith was saying, "God has called me to live, serve, and die among my people . . . even if I die early." This dear brother is willing to suffer and even die to fulfill his call to reckless faith in Jesus.

All through the history of the church, from the start until today, there have been followers of Jesus who have embraced reckless love that cost them their lives. These martyrs stood for Jesus no matter what the cost. And in their cases, the cost was their very blood. It was Jim Elliot who said, "He is no fool who gives what he cannot keep to gain what he cannot lose."[23] After penning these words, and many others that reflected a surrendered and reckless love for God, Jim was killed by the very tribal people he felt called to reach with the gospel.

Some years ago I picked up a little book called *Prayers of the Martyrs*.[24] When I want perspective and need to adjust my outlook to become more passionate about my love for God, I spend time reading these prayers. Here are some examples:

Let me be steadfast in my faith to the end.
I have no hope of seeing my brethren again in this
    life.
If they kill me, let me die as a witness to my faith;
if I live, let me go on proclaiming it.
        —*Gabra Michael*, died August 28, 1855, in
    chains because he would not deny faith in Jesus

Come fire and cross and grapplings with wild beasts,
The rending of my bones and body,
Come all the torments of the wicked one upon me.
Only let it be mine to attain unto Jesus Christ.
                —*Ignatius of Antioch*, killed by
                        wild beasts in AD 107

Blessed are you, Lord Jesus Christ, Son of God,
For you have, in your mercy, been so kind as to allow
    me a death like yours.
                —*Papylus of Thyateira*, examined,
                        tortured, and killed for being a
                    Christian in the late second century

This is the end, but for me it is only the beginning of
    life.
                —*Dietrich Bonhoeffer*, Lutheran pastor
                        executed in Nazi Germany, 1945

There is but one king that I know;
It is he that I love and worship.
If I were to be killed a thousand times for my loyalty
    to him,
I would still be his servant.
Christ is on my lips, Christ is in my heart;
no amount of suffering will take me from him.
                —*Genesius of Rome*, martyred
                        under Diocletian, AD 285

There is something about reading these prayers that ignites
the heart of a Christian.[25] When we think of these brothers

and sisters who loved to the point of death, our hearts should be filled with new passion and commitment. We should want to be more reckless and love God, no matter what the cost.

Reckless Love for God's People

When we love God, our hearts warm to the things that he loves. At the top of God's list is his church, his beloved bride.[26] The question is not, does God love the church, but do we love his church?

I did not grow up in a Christian fellowship or in a family that went to church. When I started going to church, I had no history, either good or bad, with being part of a church community. I came into the family of God with a blank slate. Over the coming years, I was amazed at how kind and loving Christians were. For the most part, they reached out to me, tried to help me figure out how to walk with Jesus, and cheered me on. A lot of them even prayed for me and encouraged me as I was growing up in the faith.

With time, I got so close to some Christians that I discovered they loved me enough to tell me when I was making a dumb choice or living in a way that did not honor God. These people actually cared enough to point out where I was messing up and helped me learn to read the Bible, make better choices, and receive the grace of God when I stumbled and fell. I have to say it, and say it loud and clear: I am a big fan of Christians!

This is why I am so troubled with the current trend to beat up the church. There seems to be growing criticism from outside the church and from inside. The dilemma, as I see it, is that the church is not some amorphous spiritual piñata that we can take a bat to anytime we like. Beating up on the church is no game. As far as I can tell from my study of the Bible, the church is the people of God. The church is you, me, and our brothers and sisters all over the world.[27] We are a body connected through faith in the Savior. We are to love each other, serve each other, rejoice in the good times, and shed tears together in the hard times.[28] There is no room for beating up on the bride of Jesus.

Let me be perfectly clear. I am aware, on a very personal level, that people in the church can be harsh, mean-spirited, and even cruel. Sometimes these tough people are wolves in sheep's clothing who have found a way into a local church fellowship.[29] At other times they are believers in Jesus, but they operate out of their own pain, brokenness, and sin. These would be people Marshall Shelley calls "Well-Intentioned Dragons."[30] In either case, if you are an active part of a local Christian fellowship of believers, there is a good chance you may end up hurt by someone who claims to be a brother or sister in Christ.

I am a local church pastor. I understand that people in the church can be cruel. I have served in the church for over three decades. I have my fair share of scars and war stories I could tell. Most of us do. But let's not focus on these. Let's turn our attention to celebrating the good and invest in strengthening the church. God would rather have us invest our energy in taking reckless chances to love the church and not let ourselves become bitter critics of Jesus's bride.

You might say, "But I have been hurt by Christians. If I seek to love the church and care for people in my local fellowship of believers, I might get hurt by them." All I can say is, "You are right. You might." Both faith and love can be reckless. There is always a chance of experiencing relational pain when we get close to people, and the more we love, the greater the chance of that happening.

Loving people in the church is a risky proposition, but it is also a glorious privilege. In the coming chapters we will look at many specific and practical ways we can take chances and extend reckless love to our brothers and sisters in Christ.

As we receive the amazing grace of God, we dare to love the people of God and connect closely with them even when this is difficult. But our adventure of reckless love does not end there. We must take things one step further. We are called to love people who are not yet aware of the grace of Jesus and the joy of being part of God's family. In the coming chapters we will also discover practical ways to bring the love of God to a hurting and broken world that desperately needs what only God can bring. Along the way, we will discover that one of the primary ways God has chosen to bring his love to the world is through you and me.

Reflections on Responsible Recklessness

Our son Josh gave Sherry a little blue box filled with every-thing his young mind could think of. On top of that, he gave himself. He bound himself to his mom with his little hand-cuffs. What a beautiful picture of reckless love!

The martyrs quoted in this chapter gave their very lives for the sake of Jesus. With deep faith in God and staggering courage, they refused to deny the Savior who had captured their hearts. This is another powerful portrait of reckless love.

The apostle Paul writes a list of the ways he willingly suffered in his service to Jesus, including receiving the forty lashes minus one on five different occasions, being beaten with rods three times, being stoned, and facing many other physical, emotional, and spiritual torments.[31]

Is the Bible teaching us that we should look for opportuni-ties to suffer? Is the message of Scripture calling Christians to embrace any and all suffering as a sign of spiritual com-mitment and maturity? Is suffering a sign of reckless love?

The Bible shows us that suffering *can* grow our faith and draw us closer to God. But the Bible does not teach us that all suffering is good or that we should always choose to suffer when the opportunity presents itself.

There are two accounts in the book of Acts that show the apostle Paul facing a situation where he was going to be beaten.[32] In each case Paul was doing his ministry, but he was not seeking to create conflict. In the first account, when Paul was ministering in the city of Philippi, he was arrested, publicly beaten, and locked in jail. Paul was a Roman citizen and the laws of Rome forbade any magistrate to treat a person this way without a trial. Had Paul spoken up, they never would have locked him up or beaten him without a trial. In the passage we see that Paul never mentioned his Roman citizenship during this time of intense suffering. He allowed them to flog him.[33]

It would be easy to read this account and conclude that Christians should learn to suffer in silence, just like Paul did. Maybe this passage is meant to teach us that suffering for the sake of Jesus is so valuable that we should invite it and not defend ourselves. Maybe reckless love means being silent during suffering, no matter what we face.

We might get this idea from the sixteenth chapter of Acts, but we see a very different story unfold in Acts 22. In this chapter Paul is once again in the middle of an unruly crowd. The Roman soldiers take him into the barracks. They stretch him out and are about to flog him. This seems like a perfect time to show his reckless love for Jesus and face another round of suffering for the sake of the gospel.

Rather than suffer in silence, Paul asks the centurion soldier a very pointed question: "Is it legal for you to flog a Roman citizen who hasn't even been found guilty?"[34] Paul and the centurion both knew the answer to this question. It was an emphatic "No!"

As the story unfolds and the Roman soldiers learn that Paul was born a Roman citizen, they become alarmed because they had put him in chains with no grounds for this action.[35] In this case, Paul claims his Roman citizenship and makes them stop before they beat him.

What is going on here? In one case Paul remains silent and is beaten. In another case he speaks up and puts a stop to the persecution. Why such different responses?

I would suggest that this has something to do with responsible recklessness. We must be prayerful and discerning in how we love people. In some situations God might call us to love to the point of suffering . . . for the sake of the gospel. If you read the full text of Acts 16, you see that a revival broke out in the prison after Paul and Silas were beaten and locked up. The jailer and his whole family placed their trust in Jesus. The suffering of Paul and Silas led to transformed lives. It was redemptive and bore fruit for the kingdom of God.

Somehow, in Acts 22 Paul had a sense that this was not a time to be beaten for the faith. It was a time to speak up, claim his citizenship, and put a stop to the impending flogging. In this case Paul did not see the kingdom value in facing another round of beatings.

How does this translate to reckless love today? We need to be very prayerful and discerning when we face potential suffering for the gospel. There might be times God calls us to embrace pain for the sake of Jesus and the advancement of his gospel. There will also be times when God makes it clear that there is not a need to suffer and it will not forward his kingdom work.

The only way we will know is if we pray, and seek God's wisdom. If you are confident that God is calling you to suffer for the sake of Jesus, do it with grace and confidence. He gave his life for you and he believed you were worth the suffering he endured.

On the other hand, if you feel released from suffering and do not believe God is calling you to face a moment of pain, then walk away from it. There is no shame in this. Suffering is only valuable when God can use it for something redemptive. Suffering for the sake of suffering is not God's plan. Be reckless for Jesus, but make sure you are responsibly reckless!

Diving into Reckless Love

>> **Praying Reckless Prayers**

Spend time on your own, or with other Christians, and pray in some of the following directions:

- Thank God for the people he has placed in your life who have been a consistent example of reckless love.
- Give praise to God for loving you before you ever loved him. Read Romans 5:6–11 and 1 John 4:7–12 and spend time rejoicing and celebrating God's seeking love that pursued you long before you ever knew who Jesus was.
- Invite God to become your best and closest friend. Identify areas of your life where you have not fully invited God to rule. Then, offer these areas to God and surrender them to his lordship.
- Think through the following four areas and identify any way that these things have taken a place of importance that is greater than they deserve. Pray that God will be first and above all else in your life, including these things:
  material things and earthly riches
  security and comfort
  the people in your life
  pride or self-interests

>> **Taking Reckless Actions**

The love of God led Jesus to the cross. He suffered willingly and gladly for us. Our love for people can mean discomfort, hurt, or even deep pain. When we feel hurt, we tend to pull back and remove ourselves from the source of pain. If there is a person God wants you to be near, but you have pulled away because of some pain you have experienced, open your heart to reconnect with this person. Pray, gain perspective, and be patient. If God affirms that you should spend time with this person and reach out to them in love, take a next step and live in obedience, even if it means facing potential or probable pain. If God does not lead you to reconnect with this person, then be at peace as you keep your distance.

≫ Thinking Reckless Thoughts

Reflect on some of these questions in the coming days:

- How has God revealed his love to me (before I was born and throughout my lifetime)?
- How have I experienced Jesus as my closest friend?
- What can I do to grow my friendship with the Savior?
- What is trying to push in and take first place in my life ahead of God? What can I do to fight back and make sure God stays central and supreme in my life?
- Where do I need to be more willing to live with discomfort or even pain for the sake of Jesus?
- Where do I need to walk away from pain because it is not accomplishing anything of value for the kingdom of God?

4

reckless generosity

He really believed his comment was funny. I think he meant it as a joke, but it bothered me every time he said it. He always had a twinkle in his eye and I could tell he was trying to bug me with his words . . . at least a little. It happened every time I preached on any topic even remotely relating to giving, money, or generosity.

I would finish the message and Larry[1] would make a beeline toward me. I knew what was coming. "Well, Pastor, I have to let you know, the batteries in my hearing aid died about halfway through your sermon today." He would chuckle and then wander off.

To be honest, I felt bad for Larry. In a roundabout way he was telling me about the condition of his heart.[2] He wanted me to know that when the topic of personal resources and generosity came up, he was shutting off . . . he was not listening . . . he wanted nothing to do with it. Larry thought he was being clever and guarding his stuff so that God could not use it or take it from him. Instead, he was missing the journey of reckless faith and the adventure that is unleashed when we learn to live a generous life.

A Journey toward Reckless Generosity

Sherry grew up in a home with parents who loved Jesus and taught her the joy of giving. She watched her dad and mom set aside the first 10 percent of their income every single week. It was a holy ritual of literally taking the first 10 percent of their income, placing the cash in an envelope, and putting it up above a cabinet in the kitchen. On Sunday this tithe (or 10 percent) was placed in the offering plate as a declaration that everything is a gift from God. It was a joyful discipline of trust in the one who gives his children every good gift.[3] On top of this, Sherry's folks would look for reasons and opportunities to share the rest of their resources as needs arose and God led them.

Two thousand miles away, on the West Coast, I was growing up in a home with very loving and generous parents, but no spiritual heritage. Though my folks often helped people in need and opened their home to many people who had nowhere to live, I never went to church or saw my parents give tithes or offerings.[4]

When Sherry and I started dating, she taught me about the value of joyfully giving the first 10 percent of our income to God's work in the church and the world. She went on to explain that everything else we have is to be held in open hands and made available for God's use as he directs . . . and this means everything.

Though I had been a follower of Jesus for about three years, I had missed the whole idea of living a financially generous life. As Sherry told me her story, how she had been raised, and her biblical convictions about giving generously, I decided I had better do some homework. I wanted to marry this woman someday and this was a big topic that demanded we be on the same page.

I dug into every passage I could find that spoke to this issue. I wanted to know what God had to say about *my* resources. It did not take long for the picture to snap into crystal-clear focus. Here is a small sample of the biblical truths that began to form my thinking:

I was wondering, does God really expect me to give him the first 10 percent of everything I earn for the rest of my life? Does he really take this generosity thing all that seriously? Is this really a big deal? Then I read:

> "Will a man rob God? Yet you rob me.
> "But you ask, 'How do we rob you?'
> "In tithes and offerings. You are under a curse—the whole nation of you—because you are robbing me. Bring the whole tithe into the storehouse, that there may be food in my house. Test me in this," says the LORD Almighty, "and see if I will not throw open the floodgates of heaven and pour out so much blessing that you will not have room enough for it. I will prevent pests from devouring your crops, and the vines in your fields will not cast their fruit," says the LORD Almighty. "Then all the nations will call you blessed, for yours will be a delightful land," says the LORD Almighty. (Mal. 3:8–12)

I needed to know what my attitude should be as I learned to give. The truth is, I was not coming at it with a whole lot of joy and excitement. Then I read,

> Remember this: Whoever sows sparingly will also reap sparingly, and whoever sows generously will also reap generously. Each man should give what he has decided in his heart to give, not reluctantly or under compulsion, for God loves a cheerful giver. And God is able to make all grace abound to you, so that in all things at all times, having all that you need, you will abound in every good work. (2 Cor. 9:6–8)

I needed clarity about my priorities when it comes to God and the stuff of this world, and these words of Jesus guided me:

No one can serve two masters. Either he will hate the one and love the other, or he will be devoted to the one and despise the other. You cannot serve both God and Money. (Matt. 6:24)

In a world that calls us to upgrade, get more, and never truly be content, the teaching of the apostle Paul gave me fresh perspective:

But godliness with contentment is great gain. For we brought nothing into the world, and we can take nothing out of it. But if we have food and clothing, we will be content with that. People who want to get rich fall into temptation and a trap and into many foolish and harmful desires that plunge men into ruin and destruction. For the love of money is a root of all kinds of evil. Some people, eager for money, have wandered from the faith and pierced themselves with many griefs. (1 Tim. 6:6–10)

I looked at my future as a pastor, husband, and dad and could see the probable financial struggles on our horizon. It was a time when interest rates for homes were over 10 percent. I received hope as I read,

I am not saying this because I am in need, for I have learned to be content whatever the circumstances. I know what it is to be in need, and I know what it is to have plenty. I have learned the secret of being content in any and every situation, whether well fed or hungry, whether living in plenty or in want. I can do everything through him who gives me strength. (Phil. 4:11–13)

With each passing year, we learned the challenge and joy of tithing, and we kept looking for ways to give beyond this starting point of 10 percent. At the same time, we worked hard to stay out of debt and even began a savings account to help our boys go to college someday. Then, things got really reckless!

Pushing the Boundaries of Recklessness

The church I served was in the beginning stages of a fund-raising program.

We desperately needed more space so we could reach more people in our community with the love and grace of Jesus. I was the lead pastor of the church and realized I would be calling the whole congregation to sacrificial giving. With this in mind, I determined the first step I needed to take was asking our church board members to pray about what they would commit to give. I proposed that each board member take time to gather with their family members, talk, pray, and discern what they would commit to this ministry expansion project.

Little did I know that about a week prior to this meeting, while Sherry was out on her morning jog, the Holy Spirit was preparing her for the call on our life to give recklessly. She told me later that as she was running and praying, she felt the Holy Spirit impressing on her heart that she was to get ready to give sacrificially. She wasn't sure what that meant at the time, but it was clear enough that she still remembers the exact spot on her run where that strong word was given.

Not knowing this piece of information at that time, I asked Sherry to meet me for lunch at our favorite Chinese restaurant. My plan was to ask her to start praying with me about how much we should give to the expansion campaign. I had already been praying about it and I had a certain amount I felt was God's call, but I knew we had to make this decision as a couple.

As we were eating our egg drop soup, I began to tell Sherry about the challenge I had given our church board. I asked her to begin praying about the specific commitment God might want us to make. At that point Sherry smiled and said that God had already been preparing her for this opportunity to be generous. She told me all about how, while she had been running, God told her to get ready to be generous. Then she looked at me and said, "As a matter of fact, God has placed a specific amount on my heart that I think we should give."

I asked her to tell me the amount because I also had a strong conviction about a specific financial commitment we should make. Sherry said, "I feel like it is a crazy amount because we just don't have this kind of money." I said, "You go first." She leaned toward me at the table and quietly said the amount.

You guessed it. It was the exact dollar figure God had impressed on me. To be honest, it really was a crazy amount for us. It was essentially our savings for the boys' college and everything else we could scrape together. We knew in that moment God was calling us to reckless generosity. We needed to give our boys' college savings away. As we did this, God put a firm conviction in our hearts that he would take care of our sons. We could trust him, because this was his idea and he was leading us.

So we did it! We gave it to God with full confidence that he held the future in his hands, and we were sure that he loves our boys more than we do.

I have never shared this story from the pulpit during a sermon and I seriously debated about telling it in this chapter of *Reckless Faith*. But this was a defining moment in our marriage and our faith.

What really surprised us was that a few years later God called us to do it again. It would happen late at night, after another board meeting, when we were headed into a new level of our church building campaign. Again, I came home and asked Sherry to join me in another round of praying for how much we should give. I guess we didn't expect God to answer so quickly, but we had the same thing happen. We both came up with the same amount. In essence, it was double the amount we had given the previous time.

God was getting ready to stretch our faith even more. This doubled amount meant we would again be giving everything we had saved and would have to come up with even more than what we had at the time. We prayed and told God that we believed he had spoken to us and we would commit to give the amount. He would have to provide. Our part was to trust in him and to work real hard.

Some people might look at what we did as irresponsible recklessness, and I would agree with them—except both Sherry and I knew that God was calling us to do this. We had a clear and corporate conviction. It was not something we came up with on our own. We would have been living in disobedience had we not given those resources to God's work.[5]

Both times God spoke to Sherry and me and put the exact same amount on our hearts and minds. We both had a firm conviction that he would provide what we needed. After the second time this happened, I can remember kneeling next to our bed as a couple and thanking God that he had been so clear with us. We knew he would provide what we committed to give, and he did. Shortly after that night, we received some extra work that paid enough for us to fulfill our commitment.

In the case of our boys' education, at the writing of this book, our oldest has graduated from a state university in Michigan with no debt for him or us. Our middle son completed his degree at a private Christian school in Southern California with no loans. And our youngest son is in his junior year at a private Christian Bible college in Spokane, Washington. To date, he also has no debt. All three of them have worked while in school and in the summers to help pay for their school. They have received some academic scholarships. And Sherry and I have helped wherever we could. When they started college, we did not have a special savings account. But over the past six years (at one point all three were in college at the same time), God has given us opportunities to do extra work that has helped cover the costs of their education.

For the record, I would never have dreamed this was the way their college would have been paid for, but God knew. He called us to be recklessly generous, and he has taken care of our needs.

Don't get me wrong. I am not one of those preachers who says, "Give God ten dollars and he will promise to give back a hundred." I believe that kind of teaching is manipulative and unbiblical. What I do believe is that we are called to be radically generous, recklessly committed to giving, and willing to live with open hands and hearts. Most of the time, when you give a hundred dollars to God's work, the net financial reality is that you have a hundred dollars less in your bank account. But if God has called you to give, he will take delight in your obedience and provide what you need.

In our case God's provision did not come through a surprise check in the mail or some inheritance from a deceased uncle I never knew. It came through God providing work projects we did in the evenings and on the weekends. We saw these as opportunities to take care of our family and grow in generosity.

Reckless and Obedient

Keith was the vice president of our church board, a passionate Christian, and the founder and owner of a successful automotive business. I remember one day, when we were talking about living a generous life, he looked at me and said, "If I were to give 10 percent of my income to ministry, I would be walking in disobedience to God." I was shocked, because I had a feeling that Keith was a generous giver. He looked at me and, with humble honesty, said, "If I give less than 50 percent of what I earn, I am robbing God." I was blown away! This kind of devotion to reckless generosity was new to me.

Over the coming years, I have watched as this man of God and his wife follow the leading of the Holy Spirit to give more and more toward the things of God. One day he told me God had called him to give up the business, go back to school, and become a pastor. I told him that this did not surprise me at all. It was a joy to see how God used the resources he had earned to cover the expenses of his family as he went to college and then seminary. Today he serves as a local church pastor and has a fruitful ministry in North Carolina. God used his example of reckless generosity to raise the bar in my life and challenge me to take bigger steps of aggressive and joyful giving.

Open Hands or Clenched Fists?

We live in a world where people hold on to their financial resources with a kung fu grip and don't want to let anything go. In a time when national and world economics are unstable at best, we can be tempted to cling to what we have with white-knuckled fury. This is not God's plan for us. He invites and calls us to a joyful life of reckless generosity. To grow more generous is the pathway to freedom and life. To cling to what we have is a trap that leads to fear, anxiety, and bondage.

Some years ago I saw a documentary about a tribe in Africa that catches monkeys in a very interesting way. You might have heard about it. Just to be sure I had the story right, I went onto YouTube and watched a few monkeys being caught with this exact technique.[6] The person wanting to capture a monkey makes a hole in a tree trunk or a coconut. The hole needs to be just big enough for the monkey to slip its hand in. Then, in the hollow space inside of the hole, they place an orange or some food the monkey enjoys. After this, they wait.

When the monkey comes and smells the tasty treat, he slips his hand into the tree and grabs the food. Here is the dilemma. Once the monkey has the food gripped in his fist, he can't withdraw his hand. He is trapped. All he has to do is open his hand and let the food go, but most do not. Monkeys will scream and pull, but they can't get free. While they are panicking, the hunter comes and captures the unsuspecting creature.

It would be easy to look at these furry primates, shake our heads, and wonder how they could be so easily trapped. But Jesus gave many warnings to us about loving money and worldly possessions so much that they trap and even destroy us. There are moments when we must look a bit like the monkey with his hand caught in the tree. If we would release our grip on the stuff of this world and live with open hands, we would find freedom and joy. Instead, we hold on with a kung fu grip and don't notice that we are trapped by our own greed.

The question becomes, what can we do to grow a heart and lifestyle of reckless generosity?

Adjusting Our Perspective

If we are going to live a recklessly generous life, we must gain a heavenly perspective on material things. The Bible does not teach that money, in and of itself, is evil. But the love of money is the starting point of all sorts of evil. Loving material things too much can actually drive us away from God and corrupt our faith.[7] We need to learn to see money and material things in a new way.

One thing that will help us form a biblical and God-honoring perspective is realizing that *everything we have is a gift from a loving heavenly Father.* Even when we work hard, our ability to work comes from God. When we use our minds, we need to remember that every ounce of intellectual prowess we have was given as a gift from God. Our physical strength is given and sustained by our Creator. Each day and every breath is only received because God chooses to give it. In the book of James we read, "Every good and perfect gift is from above, coming down from the Father of the heavenly lights, who does not change like shifting shadows" (1:17).

Every good gift is from above. It really is. When we acknowledge this, we become profoundly thankful and diligently generous. God has been good to us. How can we hoard what we have and keep it for ourselves?

Another way to adjust our perspective is by recognizing that *most of the people reading this book are actually rich.* In the scope of the whole human family, people who can afford to buy a book to read for enjoyment (or order it for their Kindle, Nook, or iPad) are among the world's wealthy. This is not to say that many of the people reading this book don't struggle with finances. What I am saying is that, when we look at the bigger picture of our world community, we will see that most of us are far better off than we often feel.

We live in a world where over three billion people—about half the world's population—live on less than $2.50 a day![8] Try to put that in perspective. When we buy a coffee or specialty drink, it costs as much or more than what half the world's people live on in an average day. When we go to a movie and buy a drink and popcorn, we spend the average amount of money that half the world's people spend in a week for everything they need. A myriad of websites give statistics about these things, and they all send the same message: those who are struggling in the United States and other developed countries are still living in luxury compared to a large majority of the people on this planet.

We look into a refrigerator filled with food and say, "There is nothing to eat." We open a closet packed full of clothes and feel discouraged that we have nothing to wear. In reality, what we should say is, "I don't have any clothes I want to wear, because they don't fit the hottest new stylistic trend." Or "I have lots of clothes in my closet, but they don't fit because I have been eating too much." In either case, our perspective is warped and we need to see things as they really are.

If I have a roof over my head (it could be a house, an apartment, or a trailer), three or four sets of clothing (most of us have far more), two or more pairs of shoes, and two or more meals a day, I am in the world's elite. That's the truth. When we understand this reality, we can become generous, because we start to understand how blessed we really are.

I have come up with a little mantra that you might want to try. It is a perspective-giving statement that might help you see your resources with new eyes. It has three parts:

1. I have a lot—
2. it is all a gift from God,
3. so it does not ultimately belong to me!

I shared this little mantra when I was speaking at Westmont College, a wonderful Christian school in Santa Barbara, California. One of the students came up to me after my talk in chapel, and he was visibly upset. He did not like my suggestion that they should say their stuff did not really belong to them. I was so glad he came up and articulated his concern, because it led to a great conversation.

I explained to him that I am not a socialist—I own a car, and I even have a house. But I do live with a profound and clear perspective that, while I have a lot, it is all a gift from God, and at the end of the day, it really all belongs to God and not me. I am called to be a steward and caretaker of God's stuff. This kind of outlook frees me to live with open hands and share joyfully. All that I have is a gift from God and belongs to him—why wouldn't I share?

One more thing to help us gain a healthy perspective when it comes to money is making a decision that *I will answer for myself and I should not police what other people have.* So often Christians spend time comparing themselves to others or worrying about how everyone else is doing in the generosity department.

Years ago, when I was a student at a Christian university in Southern California, we had a guest speaker come to chapel. In the coming years, I heard him give the same message in various contexts—he made grandiose statements that really bothered me. He really seemed to enjoy stirring the pot with extreme and absolute statements like "A Christian can't own or drive a BMW." I was only a college student at the time, but I had a sense that he was wrong.

As time has passed, I have grown more convinced that his goal was to unsettle people and get them thinking, more than give a list of what cars a Christian can and can't drive. I remember the first time I heard him make this absolute statement. My mind began to evaluate it. Could a Christian drive a used BMW with over 200,000 miles on the odometer that they bought for $2,000? Would this be permissible by God and permitted by our guest speaker? I pondered, can a Christian drive a Volvo? I mused this scenario. What if I could buy a used BMW for $2,500 or a new Ford truck for $20,000? Would God prefer that I spend the extra $17,500 so that I would not be driving a BMW and risk upsetting our chapel speaker? I wondered, is there something inherently evil or wrong with the cluster of the three consonants, BMW? Could it be that this chapel speaker was concerned about cars that came from Bavaria? I could go on and on with the things that ran through my mind. Trust me, my mind examines these kinds of absolute declarations quite rigorously.

Just for the record, in case you are wondering if this is a personal issue, I have never owned a BMW. I'm not a real car guy, so I have driven three Hyundais in a row and now have a VW. I hope this would be acceptable to my chapel speaker.

Actually, the point I would like to make is, I find it very dangerous and exceedingly unhelpful for people to declare what someone else can and should have. We are wiser if we spend our time adjusting our personal perspective and seeking to be generous with what God places in our care. We should spend less time comparing ourselves to others and declaring what they should or should not have.

About two years before the writing of this book, my mother passed away. It was a hard time for my whole family. I was still quite new as the lead pastor of Shoreline Church. The day before I would lead the funeral service for my mom, I received a call from one of the leaders of Shoreline Church in Monterey. He let me know that a group from the church would be flying down to Orange County for the day to be there with me. I was touched beyond words. Most of my closest friends lived in Michigan (I had worked and served there for the previous twenty years) and none of them could make it out on short notice for the funeral.

This group from Shoreline Church was able to come down because a friend of the church, who owns a private plane, generously offered to have his pilot fly them all down in the morning and back in the evening. I was touched by his kind offer. The group from Shoreline came and sat in the second row on the right side. Their presence was a huge support for me in one of the tough times of life. I did not evaluate whether or not this man should have a private plane. That is not my business. I was simply thankful that he was generous and used the resources God has given him to bless others.

I am not sure what my college chapel speaker would have said about someone owning a plane. Maybe it would have been fine as long as it was not a BMW. I'm not sure. What I do know is that this same man used his plane to shuttle work crews up and down the California coast, bringing them in to build a new facility for the very university I was attending when I heard the speaker condemn all BMW owners.

Rather than spending our time analyzing what everyone else has and how they use it, we would be wise to invest our energy in praying that we can have a healthy perspective about our own resources. First, all we have is a gift from our Father in heaven. Second, for most of us, if we are honest, we have a lot! Third, we should refrain from judging and analyzing others and learn to be recklessly generous with the things God has placed in our care because they do not really belong to us anyway.

Committing to Share

When our perspective begins to shift and we are convinced that our heavenly Father has been good to us, we learn to live with open hands. We loosen our kung fu grip on the stuff of this world. We are no longer clinging to material things like the monkeys trapped by their own inability to let go. Our hands fall open in front of us, and everything is available to the God who generously gives us all we have, including his love and grace.

What a glorious way to live! We don't have to be anxious that people are trying to get our stuff. We no longer wake up and go to bed obsessed with how much we have saved or lost that day. The size of our nest egg is no longer the driving force of our life. Instead, we begin to take delight in sharing the things God has placed in our care.

The apostle Paul gave this charge to followers of Jesus:

Command those who are rich in this present world not to be arrogant nor to put their hope in wealth, which is so uncertain, but to put their hope in God, who richly provides us with everything for our enjoyment. Command them to do good, to be rich in good deeds, and to be generous and willing to share. (1 Tim. 6:17–18)

If we are rich in the scope of this world, these words should speak to our hearts. Our hope is not in worldly wealth and riches but in the One who provides for our every need. We have the privilege of doing good for others, being generous, and sharing.

Imagine a life where you look for ways to use what God has placed in your hands to bring blessing, hope, and joy to others. Let your mind dream for a minute and picture a church filled with people who are committed to being rich in good deeds, to being generous, and to sharing with each other. What might happen if followers of Jesus were intentional about developing a willingness to share with each other and with a world in desperate need?

This all sounds good in theory, but it is a reckless way to live. There are risks and dangers inherent in generosity. If we share, we need to be prepared to encounter those who might take advantage of us. When we give something away, it costs us. The real question is, are the risks worth the joy of obedience and the delight of seeing God help others through us?

There are all sorts of ways to begin this lifestyle of reckless generosity and living with open hands. My niece Clara made a decision to be a person who shares, and she did this in a big way when she was only seven years old. Sometimes she would see people living on the streets, in need or begging for change. She wanted to do something to help. Her compassionate little mind began to ponder her options, and she came up with "Bags of Hope."⁹ Clara made these little bags that contain the following items: a dollar, a lifesaver mint, a granola bar, and a little note telling people about the love of Jesus. She put her siblings to work assembling the bags. Clara's dad and mom keep these in the car so that whenever they travel and see someone in need, Clara can share. Since she started this little ministry, others have asked her to provide bags for them so they can share too. What an example of getting the heart of God at a young age! Now, I keep a few Bags of Hope in my glove box and share them whenever I have a chance.

If you live in a neighborhood, you can open your house or offer help to neighbors in times of need. I am pretty sure Jesus encouraged this.[10] When a need comes up in your family, workplace, church, or community, ask yourself and God, "Should I be part of meeting this need?" The truth is, no one person has the resources to meet every need, and if you try to, it will overwhelm you. But be open and ask God, "Is this the right moment, situation, and person to help?" If he prompts you to give some of his resources that he has placed in your care . . . go for it. If he does not call you to meet a specific need, trust that God is big enough to provide someone else to meet that need. Our part is to notice, be available, ask God what we should do, and take action as he prompts us.

A Generosity Killer

On a related note, it is hard to be generous and share aggressively when we are deep in debt. The weight of debt around our neck is a generosity killer. I encourage every Christian to get out of debt as quickly as possible.[11]

Through the years I have met Christians who feel they cannot tithe, give, share, or be generous until they are debt free. Honestly, these people don't usually have a plan to get out of debt but keep digging their hole deeper and deeper over time. They are not generous but promise they will be once they get their finances in order. This is often a carrot on a stick that they talk about but never reach.

One Christian woman told me she did not give to her church, tithe, or share her resources because she was in debt. She declared, "I think it would be irresponsible for me to give because I am already in debt!" I asked her how long she had been in debt and what her plan was to get out of this financial black hole. The answer was typical. "I guess it has been about ten years. And I have no idea when I will get out of debt." She was a committed believer but had missed the call to be generous and share with others.

I challenged her: "You should start tithing today!" She looked at me like I had told her to juggle watermelons. She was noticeably confused. "But I can't afford to give anything, I am in debt!" This led to a great and vigorous conversation about priorities, setting a budget, living on less, and obedience—even when it is hard.

With time, she made a plan to get out of debt and begin sharing from the limited resources she had, and her heart began to change. As she experienced the inexpressible delight of sharing the resources God had given her, she finally realized that she had been hiding behind an excuse of debt and squandering all of her resources on herself.

Learning Contentment

Contentment is a word that rarely graces our conversations these days. The concept is becoming foreign. When we say it, some people stare as if we are speaking a foreign language. The word that embodies this attitude is "Enough!"—a simple word that reveals the presence of contentment . . . yet another virtue that has fallen on hard times.

We live in an upgrade society where we always feel the need for the newer, better, faster, larger (or smaller) version of what we already have. The idea of keeping and using things that are no longer in style is painful for some. The notion that we can keep an old version of something for months or years after the newer version has hit the market seems almost wrong to some people. Even when the economy is sluggish or stalled, the desire to upgrade to the latest and greatest is at the front of many people's minds.

An attitude of contentment says, "I have enough! I am actually happy with where I am and what I have. I don't need, or particularly want, something more than what I have today."

Just for the record, this pathological discontent is nothing new. As long as people have walked on this earth, contentment has been a virtue that far too few people embrace. But it is a key to reckless generosity. When we grow content with what we have, we posture ourselves to become far more generous than we could ever be when we are addicted to having more, more, more.

I was serving my first church out of seminary and learning the joys and complexities of local congregational ministry. The chair of our deacon's board invited Sherry and me over for dinner with him and his wife. We arrived anticipating a wonderful evening with these new friends. As I pulled up to their house, I was a little confused. This couple lived in a nice, but modest, double-wide mobile home. I knew that both of them worked full-time and had jobs that must have paid fairly well, but they lived in a very simple home.

I am embarrassed to say it, but I found myself wondering why they lived there instead of in a neighborhood more befitting their income. I was wise enough to keep my thoughts to myself through the whole evening. But a few months later as we got to know each other better, I asked my new friend why he and his wife lived in such a modest place. I inquired if they ever thought of upgrading.

He did not scold me or even give me a condescending look. He thought for a moment and then explained, "We have often thought about upgrading and moving to a bigger place. But every time we talk about it, we realize that if we do this, we could not give as much away. To tell the truth, we are perfectly happy here. We have everything we need."

I was embarrassed and humbled by his response. I will never forget that moment. Over the coming years I watched this man and woman model deep contentment and reckless generosity. They gave and gave with joy and freedom. Their contentment with what they had and where they lived unleashed them to the kind of reckless faith I have seen few times before or since.

Look again at the apostle Paul's words:

> But godliness with contentment is great gain. For we brought nothing into the world, and we can take nothing out of it. But if we have food and clothing, we will be content with that. (1 Tim. 6:6–8)

The lifeblood of contentment is not what we have but who we know. If you have an authentic friendship with Jesus, you can be content, because you have everything that matters most in the universe. Contentment is not about being rich or poor in the eyes of the world. The richest people can be discontent, while a person with very little in the eyes of the world can be completely content.

What Does Contentment Look Like?

Before Sherry and I got married, I told her there was a very good chance we would never own a house. She had grown up in West Michigan where couples would get married and routinely buy a cute little "starter house" before the wedding day. Homes were much more reasonable there than where we were living. We were serving a church in Glendora, California, where the rent on a small two-bedroom apartment was substantially more than the mortgage payments on a house in Michigan. This was a big shift in thinking for a Michigan girl, but Sherry joyfully agreed that she would be fine with living in an apartment . . . indefinitely if that was what needed to happen.

Over the next few years we lived in a little single-bedroom unit of a triplex in Pasadena. According to the guy who helped us with our taxes, we lived below the poverty line for three years. Our first son was "born into poverty," according to American economics. The truth is, we had no idea we were poor—we thought we were rich. We were happy. We had everything we could possibly need.

Next we moved into a two-bedroom apartment in Glendora, just a short drive from the church. There was a community pool, a little playground near the back of the complex, and very sweet neighbors. We were content. We were happy! We had everything we could possibly need.

When we moved to Michigan for me to do a doctoral program and serve Zion Reformed Church in Grandville, Michigan, we lived in a parsonage (a church-owned house). We were thrilled! We actually had room for our growing family of four (and five by the time we moved from that home). We had a little backyard and two big oak trees in the front. In the fall we would rake the leaves into big piles and watch our boys jump into them. We were happy! We had everything we could possibly need.

When I was called to be lead pastor at Corinth Church in Byron Center, Michigan, where I would end up serving for about fourteen years, they offered to help us get our own home. They gave us a loan for the down payment (because we still did not have enough money to consider buying a home . . . even in Michigan). My wonderful Michigan wife, who agreed to never have a house of her own if this is what God wanted for us, was delighted as we moved to a simple Cape Cod–style home at the end of a cul-de-sac on a little pond. When we moved into that house, we were happy! We had everything we could possibly need.

Do you get the point? An apartment, a parsonage, or a house did not make us happy. Jesus made us happy. These were just places we lived our faith and sought to serve God. Being content is not based on what we have or where we live;

it is a condition of the heart. When we are content, we can be generous in any location or condition.

Focusing on Eternity

One more way to grow in reckless generosity is learning to see the world with eternal eyes. Some things last forever and everything else is temporary. The list of what lasts forever is pretty short. This is what I come up with: God, the things of God (including his Word[12]), and people. That's about it. Everything else we invest in is really transitory.

Jesus wanted us to see the world this way when he taught:

> Do not store up for yourselves treasures on earth, where moth and rust destroy, and where thieves break in and steal. But store up for yourselves treasures in heaven, where moth and rust do not destroy, and where thieves do not break in and steal. For where your treasure is, there your heart will be also. (Matt. 6:19–21)

There are some things we invest in that rust, rot, and can be stolen. There are other things that are stamped "Eternal" by God and last forever. If we get this right, we make a shift in our thinking, investments, and lifestyle. We find ourselves pouring our time, energy, and resources into the things of God and the people around us. These are the heavenly treasures that don't ever pass away.

Imagine an elderly woman drawing near the end of her life. The doctors have told her she has hours or days left before she dies. She has been released from the hospital and has gone to stay at her daughter's house, because the doctors have been clear there is nothing else they can do. Picture this woman lying in bed and asking if someone can drive to her apartment across town and bring back all her jewelry, shoes, and dresses so she can take one more look at them.

It's hard to picture because it would never happen!

In this moment, she would not be using the time and breath she still has to examine a string of pearls or admire a beautiful gown. She might use these precious hours to talk with her seven-year-old granddaughter; she would want to look at her six-month-old grandson one more time. She might want to have a conversation with her daughter. Hopefully she would want to have a pastor visit for prayer. She might want to hear some Scripture read. These are the things that matter because these have the feel, smell, and touch of eternity. These are what matter forever.

Reckless faith shows itself in a generous spirit and life. We learn to live with open hands as we adjust our perspective and discover that we have a lot—it is all a gift from God, and it is to be used for his glory. Our lifestyle reflects the heart of God when we commit to be people who share what God has placed in our hands rather than hold on to it with a kung fu grip. We feel freed to give and share when we discover the power of contentment and begin declaring that forgotten word, "Enough!" And when our eyes are fixed on what lasts forever, we find ourselves investing in the things of God and the people around us, because they are eternal and nothing else is. This is the road to reckless generosity.

Reflections on Responsible Recklessness

It would be easy to read this chapter and reflect on these biblical passages and feel that every need we encounter demands that we give. The truth is, God wants us to be open, available, and responsive, but he will not call us to meet every need we see. We simply don't have the resources, and sometimes wisdom would call us to refrain from giving. This is why we must use the matrix for responsible recklessness: pray, get perspective, and be patient. When we do this, we just might avoid some of the dangerous pitfalls that come when we are generous without discernment.

An experience I had years ago became a powerful object lesson for me. As I pulled into the driveway of the triplex where I lived in Pasadena, California, I saw two police cars parked near the back apartment where my grandmother lived. My heart sank. I hurried back to her unit, my heart racing, my mind wondering what had happened.

When I saw my grandmother sitting at her kitchen table, seemingly unharmed, I breathed a sigh of relief. I introduced myself and one of the officers explained, with blunt brevity, "One of your friends robbed and assaulted your grandmother."

I stood there in shock, my eyes fixed on my grandmother as she sat with her eyes turned to the ground. My mind raced to put the pieces together. The officer filled in the blanks and then it all made sense.

This moment was one of my first lessons of reckless generosity gone wrong. To understand what happened, we have to turn the clock back to the morning of that same day.[13]

A young man had come knocking on my door asking for food, clothes, and a place to take a nap. This was not unusual in my neighborhood. In Pasadena there are very nice areas, and very rough areas. I did not live on the good side of the tracks. Over the past year I had helped out various people who had passed by, knocked on my door, or caught me walking into my small front apartment. In each case, I did whatever I could. I opened my closet and let people take clothes. I gave money, when I had it. I provided food—often it was Top Ramen noodles because I had a lot of them. I was doing everything I could to follow Jesus's call to love the hurting and provide for the poor. If I had two of something, I felt I had to give to anyone who had none.[14]

This particular day a guy in his early twenties had crashed on my couch for a couple of hours, eaten some food, and picked out some clothes from my closet. Most of the time he was at my house, I was at my desk doing homework for a seminary class. When I had to head off to school for an exam, he asked if he could stay and relax in the apartment while I was gone. I knew this was a risky proposition, so I told him when I would be home and let him know he could come back later.

While I was gone at school, he wandered back two units to my grandmother's place and knocked on her door. He introduced himself as a friend of mine, said he was staying at my place, and asked if he could use her bathroom. He knew my name and she assumed he was a friend and a safe person. Once he was in her house, he stole a number of things from her bedroom, and before he left, he hugged her, kissed her, and scared her in a huge way. She later told me that she truly feared he was going to do far worse to her.

By God's grace, he took what he had, left, and did no more harm. We never saw him again.

This was a moment when the need for responsible recklessness pierced my heart like a sword. In my zeal and commitment to take risks for Jesus, I had endangered one of my family members. I had not really taken time to pray for wisdom, gain perspective, or be patient. If I would have prayed, wisdom might have led me to help but with safer boundaries. If I had asked a few Christian friends for perspective, they probably would have steered me in a different direction. There were a number of great organizations near my house that helped people in need and they could have helped him. I could have given them the resources and let them do what they are equipped to do. Had I been patient and really thought through the possible implications, I might have helped meet the needs without endangering my grandmother.

Part of me wishes that everyone with a need could just be helped. Unfortunately there are times when generosity is not the right course of action. In some cases, like with my grandmother, my reckless generosity hurt another person. There are even cases when being generous can hurt the person we are trying to help. This very topic is addressed in a powerful book called *When Helping Hurts*.[15]

As we grow in reckless generosity we also need to increase in wisdom. This will come as we are responsibly reckless.

Diving into Reckless Generosity

>> Praying Reckless Prayers

Spend time on your own, or with other Christians, and pray in some of the following directions:

- God of the universe, remind me each day that all I have is a gift from you.
- Jesus, you opened your hands and took the nails on the cross as you gave your life for me. Teach me how to live with open hands and an open heart. Teach me to be generous like you have been.
- I confess that I can be safe and guarded with the material things that are in my care. Teach me reckless generosity for your glory.
- Please give me an honest, humble, and heavenly perspective on what I have. Help me see the riches you have given me both spiritually and in material things.
- Teach me to have a content heart and a passion to share the things you have placed in my care.

>> Taking Reckless Actions

Try this simple exercise. Make thirty to forty small labels with these words on them: *God's stuff.* Then, prayerfully and intentionally place these labels or stickers on your favorite things. It could be on the dashboard of your car, on the case of a musical instrument, on a bookshelf where you have your favorite books, on the front door where you live, on your closet door, on your computer, on your checkbook, on your purse or wallet, or on anything else you value.

Let the presence of this little visual reminder do two things. First, let it influence your thinking about stuff. Each time you see one of these labels, say to yourself, "I have a lot . . . it is all a gift from God . . . at the end of the day, it is not mine!" Second, if someone asks you why there is a label on your dashboard or wallet or iPhone that says "God's stuff," tell them about how you are seeking to adjust your perspective when it comes to the stuff of this world.

>> Thinking Reckless Thoughts

Reflect on some of these questions in the coming days:

- What has God placed in my care, and am I holding these things tightly with a kung fu grip or loosely in open hands?
- Do I look at the things that are in my care as God's or mine? How is my perspective impacting my generosity?
- When was the last time I really looked for an occasion to give something away and be generous? What is getting in the way of me growing more generous?
- Do I have the sickness of our generation that demands more and more, bigger and better, and constant upgrades? How can contentment be an antidote to this poison in the soul?
- How can I invest more time, energy, and resources into things that will last forever (God and people)?

5

reckless service

From the time our middle son, Josh, was fourteen, he had a passion for communication through video. In particular he had an interest in documentaries. He loved telling stories that would make a difference for the kingdom of God. Josh had a clear sense that video would be his way of serving the world and the church. When he graduated from high school and asked us about an opportunity to go to Africa to make a documentary on a village in Zambia that was being devastated by AIDS, we were not surprised.

Josh was not asking us to go with him. He was not looking for financial support or even praise for his desire to take this risk for Jesus. He just wanted a parental thumbs-up so he could start planning for his ministry trip.

We could hear it in his voice and see it in his eyes—Josh was hungry to take a risk, stretch himself, and do something reckless for God. He was excited to go to the other side of the planet and capture a story that could increase Christians' compassion for the countless people being ravaged by the AIDS pandemic.

Our son had been serving at another local church, developing videos for worship services. This ministry was relatively tame. Now he was preparing to travel across the planet with a small team of Christians who would be serving in a place fraught with potential dangers and risks. Josh did not see this experience as heroic or out of the ordinary. It made sense to him. It fit.

Months after Josh had come home and spent a few hundred hours in post-production, we sat to watch the documentary. The title was one simple word: *LUFUTUKO*[1] (which means "God is salvation"). The film begins at a funeral in the small village, a reminder of the cost of AIDS in that faraway part of the world. The screen is pitch black. Then you hear it. Wailing. Mourning. Cries of anguish.

If you have never heard people crying at a funeral with heart-piercing sorrow and lament, it sends chills to the core of your soul. From this opening funeral scene to the hope-filled conclusion, God speaks through this short film. Five different people from that region of the world, each touched by AIDS in some way, tell their story. It is deeply moving.

When I watched the completed documentary, I knew God had blessed my son's reckless journey to Africa. I asked myself, if Josh had not returned from this trip, would I still have been sure it was the right thing to do? I know it was. This was Josh's way of serving. It was an example of his commitment to use the gifts he has been given by God to extend humble service to those who could not tell their own story to an audience in the United States.

By God's grace this video impacted many Christians in the United States. It even inspired a top automotive executive to invest time and money in the invention and development of a new technology that will help people in Zambia build a stronger economy and healthier future.[2] In addition this short film gained recognition and won an award at a film festival.[3] When we went to see *LUFUTUKO* at the festival, it was very telling. Some of the other films that had won awards at the festival included nudity, profanity, and material inappropriate for children. After Josh's film concluded, there was a sober hush in the theatre. It was a truly sacred moment. Then one of the hosts came to the front and warned everyone that the content in the next four films was not appropriate for many in the audience. Some of the families and children left the theatre at that time. It was a powerful reminder of the need to have a strong Christian witness, through film, in a secular setting.

It would have been so easy for us to discourage our son from taking the risk of going all the way to Zambia on this service project. We knew there were many risks involved. We also had a clear sense that this was an act of reckless faith and passionate service on the part of our son. We cheered on his willingness to take chances for the sake of serving others in the name of Jesus.

There is a beautiful addendum to this story. On this ministry trip to Zambia, God set the trajectory for our son's life. Josh already knew he loved production and storytelling through film. On this trip he felt a special calling to invest a big part of his attention and energy to help organizations tell their stories in compelling ways through documentary. In the year before the writing of this book, Josh worked on a documentary telling the story of land mine removal in Cambodia. Members of the US State Department have seen this film.[4] In the year after the writing of this book, he will be traveling to Guatemala to begin a documentary on medical ministry happening among the poorest of the poor.[5]

Through one decision to follow the leading of the Holy Spirit and pursue a reckless commitment to service, our son has been launched into a life of reckless adventures for Jesus. As my wife and I look on, we take delight that our son (at the writing of this book, he is only twenty-two years old) has a clear life direction that involves being adventurous, serving Jesus, and helping the world. What could be better!

The Example of Jesus

Jesus not only calls his followers to reckless service, he modeled it for us. Jesus declared of himself, "For even the Son of man did not come to be served, but to serve, and to give his life as a ransom for many."[6] In the Gospel of John we read this account:

> When he had finished washing their feet, he put on his clothes and returned to his place. "Do you understand what I have done for you?" he asked them. "You call me 'Teacher' and 'Lord,' and rightly so, for that is what I am. Now that I, your Lord and Teacher, have washed your feet, you also should wash one another's feet. I have set you an example that you should do as I have done for you. I tell you the truth, no servant is greater than his master, nor is a messenger greater than the one who sent him. Now that you know these things, you will be blessed if you do them." (John 13:12–17)

One by one they walked into the room. It was evening and they were going to share a meal with Jesus. None of them knew . . . how could they? This would become what people centuries later would call "The Last Supper."

It was the time of Passover, and each of the disciples was excited to gather with Jesus and their closest friends and remember the high point of their religious and national history. The Passover was when every family would dig back into their religious memory and revel in the reality of God's saving power. At the Passover table, they would hold in their hands the elements of a meal that reminded them of God's intervention centuries before when they were set free from slavery in Egypt. They remembered the lamb that was slain, the blood that was placed on the doorpost so the angel of death would pass over their homes, the protection this afforded each family of Israel, the journey out of Egypt, the crossing of the Red Sea, and the freedom God won for his people. This is what Jesus and his small band of disciples were gathering to celebrate at that Passover meal.

One by one the disciples walked into that upper room to do what they had done every year of their lives. They would celebrate and remember the Lord's Passover.

One by one the disciples entered that room to gather with their friend Jesus.

One by one, as they entered that upper room, each one passed by a basin and towel sitting in plain view.

What the disciples knew (that most of us do not) is why this basin and towel were sitting by the door. In the ancient world, a place of dusty roads and sandaled feet, there would often be a servant waiting by the door when a group would gather. The job of this servant was to wash the feet of weary travelers, to clean and refresh the feet of those who entered. This servant would then take the towel and dry their feet.

This was a common practice in the ancient world.

If, by chance, a group was meeting and there was no servant present for this menial chore, one of the guests who arrived early would often offer this service to the others. It would be voluntary. It was the way things were done two thousand years ago in the part of the world where Jesus and his disciples lived and traveled.

One by one the followers of Jesus entered the upper room, one by one they walked by the bowl and the towel, one by one they took their place at the table . . . with dirty feet.

Jesus noticed. He always does. That's just the way God is. He can't help but notice.

Jesus could see the basin and towel sitting, unused, by the door. He took note that all the disciples were at the table with dirty feet. He noticed that none of his followers had offered to wash the feet of their friends and partners in ministry. And none of them had offered to wash the feet of their Rabbi.

So, he got up from the table and, one by one, washed their feet.

Jesus, the Lord of Glory.
Jesus, the King of all kings.

Jesus, the One to whom every knee will bow and every tongue confess.[7]

Jesus, the One who scattered the stars into the infinite expanse of the sky.

This Jesus, one by one, washed the feet of a sinful and rebellious bunch of men who still did not fully comprehend who he was. Jesus humbly washed the feet of a group of men who had not yet learned who they were meant to be.

The high and exalted Lord of heaven knelt down at their feet, one by one, and washed them. Then, he took the towel that he had wrapped around his waist, just like an ordinary servant, and he tenderly dried their feet.

Jesus embraced the role of a servant as he washed the feet of one disciple who would soon deny that he even knew Jesus. Peter protested, but Jesus washed his feet nonetheless.

Jesus took the feet of another disciple who would soon betray him. He did not pass over the feet of Judas. He did not glare at him with anticipatory resentment. Instead, the One who would soon die for the sins of humanity washed the feet of the very man who would turn against him and betray him for thirty pieces of silver.[8]

Jesus washed the feet of the one who would soon doubt the power of the Savior to rise from the dead. He came to Thomas and gently scrubbed the caked dirt from his feet and between his toes.

One by one Jesus washed their feet, taking on the form and function of a humble servant. What recklessness! What a risk! What a Savior!

Jesus did not scold his followers for missing the moment. He did not give a lecture about how they had failed to serve each other or him. What he did was model reckless service. Jesus showed his disciples what should be normative in the life of a person who follows and seeks to be like him.

After washing each of their feet, drying them, and reclining back at the table, Jesus spoke. "You call me 'Teacher' and

'Lord,' and rightly so, for that is what I am. Now that I, your Lord and Teacher, have washed your feet, you also should wash one another's feet. I have set you an example that you should do as I have done for you."[9]

You do not have to be a Bible scholar to figure out what Jesus is driving home. The message to his followers, then and now, is clear. Bold, humble, reckless service is simply part of the deal. It is what Christians do.

We wash the feet of betrayers, doubters, deniers, friends—anyone who sits at the table with the dust of this world still caked between their toes.

We serve. It was the identity of our Savior, so it becomes our holy ambition.

We do not just take an occasional detour into the world of service. We become servants. We don't simply get involved in a service project once a year or once a month to check that off our list of spiritual obligations. Instead, we invite the Spirit of God who dwells in us to change us from self-centered and myopic consumers of religious goods to humble servants who are willing to go where the Savior went and do what the Savior did.

This kind of passionate service is an example of reckless faith. Jesus served with staggering abandon and shocking humility. So should we.

The Where, When, and How of Reckless Service

The call is clear. We are to serve with reckless passion and radical commitment. The challenge is that God does not give a set template and rigid checklist to follow. For my son Josh, reckless service took him to Zambia, Africa. For you it might mean walking across the street to help a neighbor fix a car or care for a child in a time of need. The where, when, and how of reckless service is Spirit-led and dynamic.

There are circles of influence and impact that each of us should think and pray about when it comes to a life of Christlike service. We can identify possible activities and attitudes that will propel us forward into a lifestyle of reckless service.

Circle One: Serving Where You Live

Where do you live? Where has God placed you? It could be an apartment, a tract home, a condo, military barracks, or a trailer park. Wherever it is, this is a sacred space of reckless service. If you are a follower of Jesus, your foot-washing assignment begins where you live. Too many Christians prepare for a mission trip on the other side of the world while forgetting there are service projects to be done where they sleep at night, eat breakfast, and spend their free time.

When was the last time you looked at your home as a place of ministry? What might happen if husbands committed to serve their wives, as God calls them to?[10] What might a home look like if a little brother told his big sister, "This Saturday I blocked out an hour to do an in-home service project. Would you please give me a list of things I could do to serve you?" How might this action and attitude of reckless service impact sibling relationships? When a roommate stops taking advantage of those who live in their apartment and begins to extend regular, intentional, reckless acts of service, how might the very atmosphere of the apartment change? What might our homes look and feel like if each follower of Jesus stopped focusing on "getting what I need," and became a humble and intentional servant?

Imagine this argument erupting in your living room. "No, you take the remote control, let's watch what you like." "No, no! I know that your favorite show is on right now. Let's watch what you would enjoy." "No, I insist, I would love to sit and enjoy whatever you want to watch!" As strange as this might seem, this is a small example of what could happen if we choose to serve each other rather than demand what we want.

I remember when my sister Gretchen became a Christian. She was the first of the five children in our family to give her heart to Jesus and enter a life-giving friendship with the Savior. I was only fifteen and Gretchen's newfound faith was both fascinating and irritating. She changed. She was kinder. She seemed to care about me. And she actually offered to serve me.

I had no point of reference for this behavior. It bugged me because I did not know what was motivating her. Over time, as I received consistent love and service from my sister, I was attracted to her new lifestyle. It was compelling. I did not understand what drove Gretchen to serve and care for me until I became a follower of Jesus. When I learned about the sacrifice of Jesus on the cross, his foot washing, the way Jesus cared for the outcast and broken, and all the ways the Savior served people, I began to see the vision for reckless service in the life of his followers.

What could reckless service look like in your home? It could be as simple as slowing down and listening to a family member or roommate when they are hurting. It could be a decision to make the interests of those you live with more of a priority than your own desires at critical moments. Maybe you could identify some ongoing chore that a person in your home does, but they do not enjoy, and you could do this for them. Reckless service in your home can come in a hundred different shapes and forms.

Several years ago I went to one of the early Promise Keepers gatherings in Detroit, Michigan.[11] On the way home the men on the bus were talking about the commitments they had made at this event. One challenge was to extend an act of service to your wife that would surprise and bless her. One man said, "I have decided to give my wife the whole morning next Saturday to do any chores she wants." The other guys on the bus gave a masculine grunt of approval. Another guy said he was going to give his wife free massages for a week. The ensuing ribbing and comments from the guys revealed that most of us thought his "act of service" might have had a "hidden" goal that served him . . . but who knows? After a number of people told about their plan for a home-based service project, someone asked me, "Hey, Pastor, what are you going to do for Sherry?"

My first response was to say, "I think I might have overshot on this one." I went on to explain that I could tell that Sherry did not really like making the bed, though she had done it for our whole marriage. I made a commitment to make our bed each morning—not for a week, a month, or a year, but for the rest of my life! There was a corporate groan that ran through the bus. I went on to explain that my wife likes pillows and there is a whole bunch of decorative pillows that have to go in the right place after the bed is officially made. In addition, I committed to pray for my wife every morning as I made the bed.

As of the writing of this book, and I did the math, I have made the bed over 5,000 times and spent these moments praying for my wife. I straighten the sheets and pull them nice and tight, and ask God to fill Sherry with his Holy Spirit. I get the blanket and quilt nice and smooth and tuck things in as I pray for the fruit of the Spirit to grow in my wife. I spend the needed time to get all the pillows in the right place and thank God for the gift of my wife. This simple and repetitive act of service is a powerful start to each new day. It puts things in perspective. I have discovered that even when I travel, I always make the bed and pray for Sherry—in a hotel when I know they will be making it over again. This has become part of the rhythm of my life and I am thankful for it.

The first circle of service is right where we live. I can't tell you what specific acts of service to offer to the people in your home any more than the leaders at Promise Keepers could have known that I needed to make the bed for my wife . . . for the rest of my life. But if you ask God to stir your heart and if you think about what would encourage and bless the people in your home, you will know what to do. As we learn to serve in this first circle, we will be propelled to move out to larger circles of impact.

Circle Two: Serving in Your Neighborhood

For more than a dozen years, Sherry and I lived in a neighborhood in Byron Center, Michigan. Along with our three sons, we saw our home as a lighthouse shining the presence and love of Jesus outward to our neighbors, the friends of our children, and all those who lived near us.[12] A big part of our relational connection in our neighborhood related to simple, consistent, reckless service. We let people know that we were there and available to help when needed. We looked for reasons to serve. Our home would become a place of foot washing in a modern world.

Imagine if every follower of Jesus looked at their neighborhood and all the people who live near them as a place of service. What might happen if we saw our home as a service center? What would it look like if our neighbors knew that when trouble came, our door was open? What might happen if the light of Jesus was to shine through consistent, simple, and humble acts of service? How might our neighborhoods be transformed if people knew that in the good moments and terrifying times of life, the light was on, the door was open, prayer was available, the food was hot, and your arms were spread wide with a loving welcome?

An atmosphere of reckless service can be offered in any neighborhood. Whether you're urban, suburban, or rural— whether you live in an apartment complex, in a trailer park, on a military base, in a huge estate, or even at a campground—you can create a place of loving and reckless service. It is not a matter of the kind of dwelling but the condition of our heart.

When this spirit of service and the Holy Spirit of God fill a home, it always spills over and impacts the surrounding area. Over the course of a dozen-plus years in our Byron Center home, I was amazed by what happened in our neighborhood. When a family on our street had a gathering or party, our oven and kitchen were offered, along with our time and hands. Neighbors freely walked in and out of our house, sharing our appliances and space. This became so common in our neighborhood that it spread beyond our house, and all the neighbors began sharing freely. Everyone on our Richfield Court cul-de-sac became a big family and opened their homes and lives to each other. We became a community. We became friends.

Our yards were shared space. The trampoline in our backyard became a play spot for kids in the neighborhood (with permission and safety rules). The pool became a gathering place on muggy summer days. If someone was away, the other neighbors watched out for their house, watered plants, and helped in any way they could. Our neighborhood became like a family who loved each other, played together, and served one another. I am convinced that the major catalyst for this wonderful culture was the act of serving people in the name of Jesus!

As time went on, the service took deeper and richer forms. When crisis hit, we gathered together to talk, cry, pray, and help each other. When one family would have a great moment, the rest of us would celebrate and rejoice with them. When uncertainty about a job, child, or life situation would loom over one home like a dark cloud, the rest of us would gather to offer wisdom, comfort, and tangible support. It was a glorious season of life among people we grew to love and appreciate.

Serving in our neighborhood can be reckless, because opening our heart, home, garage, and life to others always involves risk. Reckless service involves allowing ourselves to be used and taken advantage of. Our stuff can get broken, marred, or even stolen! Our kindness can be taken for granted. And the truth is, these things happen. The question is, will we take the risk of serving our neighbors in the name of Jesus, even with the possibility of tough consequences? Will we wash the feet of those who live around us even when they might not understand or appreciate our acts of service? If we do, we just might see God create a community of love and grace around us.

Circle Three: Serving in Your Workplace or at Your School

Most of us spend a great deal of time either in the workplace or a school setting. These are uniquely wonderful places to serve. In these formal settings, there are clear expectations, and when we serve in unexpected ways, the presence of Jesus is seen and felt.

One of my very first jobs was at a fast-food restaurant. This particular chain was family-owned, and they had a standard of cleanliness that greatly surpassed the federal guidelines. They even required that the floor drains be cleaned and scrubbed every day! This job was reserved for the most recently hired employee. This meant it was my job, every day I worked, until someone else was hired and they began their dreaded floor-drain initiation.

All day long the sludge and garbage that fell on the floor of the restaurant was swept and pushed into these drains. By the end of the day the drains were more sticky and vile than the floor of a movie theatre. They were particularly tricky to clean because half the drain was right along the base of the counter in the kitchen area and the other half was wedged under the counter. To clean these disgusting nooks filled with grime and all the day's food shrapnel meant getting down on your knees, with one elbow on the floor, and first scooping out all that had gathered in the drain. As I write these words, the memory banks of my mind can recall the unique sour smell of a floor drain that is unlike anything else I have ever experienced. Cleaning a floor drain meant scrubbing the white porcelain until it was shining. This was the shift-ending ritual I engaged in until the next "newest employee" would come along and I could pass the mantle.

I was a fairly new Christian when I engaged in my purgatorial floor-drain-cleaning ritual day after day. One morning, as I read my Bible, I came across this powerful little verse that transformed my attitude and the way I cleaned floor drains. This was the verse that impacted the way I served at work . . . and many other places: "And whatever you do, whether in word or deed, do it all in the name of the Lord Jesus, giving thanks to God the Father through him."[13]

I decided I would clean the floor drains in the name of Jesus—as if they were his floor drains. I would give thanks. I would not whine or complain. People noticed that attitude and were shocked. When a couple of new people were hired, my role was to train them in cleaning the floor drains and then happily walk away from this job forever.

This was my dilemma.

I knew, with all my heart, that God wanted me to keep cleaning floor drains. As strange as this sounds, it was good for my soul. I trained the new employees, but offered to clean the drains in partnership with them. At the end of each shift, we would get on our knees and elbows together and scrub the drains until they would shine.

Apparently, in the recorded history of this fast-food restaurant, my behavior was unprecedented. The manager pulled me aside and explained that I did not have to clean floor drains anymore. I had "served my time." I let him know that I was aware of this, but I was glad to help clean them whenever I was needed. He was baffled, but intrigued.

About a week later he talked to me about becoming an assistant manager. It turns out I was too young for this promotion, but the people I worked with were so confused and impressed with the whole floor drain thing that it created wonderful opportunities to talk about why I was glad and willing to serve in this way. Reckless service led to reckless words about Jesus!

Acts of service in your workplace or school setting don't have to be huge. They can be as small as scrubbing a floor drain, offering to help another student who is struggling in a class you are taking, working a little longer and harder and not asking for extra pay—anything God places on your heart. Many of us spend large portions of our time in work and school settings, and there are countless ways we can serve. These reckless gestures stand out in a world where many people do the least they can to get by. Humble foot-washing service, of any sort, reveals the presence of Jesus and opens the door for God to show up in our actions, attitudes, and even in our words.

Circle Four: Serving in Your Community

Our acts of service can be done one-on-one, but also in community with other Christians. Your local church should be engaged in acts of reckless service all around your community. In recent years it has become popular to ask the question, *If your church were to disappear tomorrow, would anyone in your community notice?* The point is simple—is your congregation serving only itself or truly engaging in ministry to those outside of the church family?

At Shoreline Community Church we have a ministry team that mobilizes hundreds of people to serve in our community.[14] Every week there are numerous ways the people of the church volunteer and serve. Twice a week we have a food pantry that offers groceries to people in need. Twice a week another group opens the doors to help people find good, clean clothes. We have teams of volunteers who lead worship services in convalescent homes for those who simply can't get out and come to church. We bring the church to them. Volunteers clean up local parks so children in the community have a good place to play and families can gather. Another team visits local shelters and cares for women who are facing very difficult challenges. They bring the grace and hope of Jesus. Yet another team of people works with an I-Help group and hosts homeless men overnight in our church facility. These are just a small sample of the ways a local church can serve the community.

Every local church should be engaged in reckless service to their community. Most of these activities cost time, energy, and resources. From a strictly human and financial vantage point, these ministries often don't "pay off." But if we look through the eyes of Jesus, they reap priceless rewards. We are foot washers, servants, and humble floor drain scrubbers. It is what we do . . . for the sake of the One who washed our feet.

Before we move on to the final circle of serving, I must tell an amazing story about a miracle that happened in one of our community outreach service ministries.

A wonderful team of servants gathers every Tuesday and Thursday and opens a free clothing service to our community. It is filled with lots of items donated by church people who have a heart to help people in need. One day a woman named Lupe came to see if she could find some clothes. She not only found articles of clothing she could use, but made friends with the loving folks who were serving at the clothing closet. She came back again and stayed around to visit her new friends. With time, Lupe began to volunteer at the clothing ministry, and she started serving others in the community. She was not a follower of Jesus but was so touched by the grace and humble service she had received, she wanted to give back. Over time, the other volunteers invited Lupe to church at Shoreline. She came and loved it! She felt something real and authentic among all these people she had just met.

One Sunday morning, about thirty minutes after the third service, I met Lupe. I had finished interacting with the last person waiting to talk and pray with me. I looked around the worship center and almost everyone was gone. I noticed a woman standing shyly off to the left side of the worship center about six rows back. I made eye contact and asked her if she was waiting for me. She nodded her head in affirmation.

I hopped off the edge of the stage where I sit to chat and pray with people after each service. I walked over to talk with Lupe and met her for the first time. After we introduced ourselves, I asked her, "What can I do for you?" She replied gently, but firmly, "I want to know Jesus!"

We sat together, talked about Jesus, and I had the delight of praying with my new sister in faith as she received the life-changing grace of the Savior. Today, Lupe leads our clothing closet ministry. She loves Jesus and extends the service she once received. Lupe offers this service with gentle, kind, reckless passion. If you were to meet this sweet sister in the faith, you would hear her repeat a refrain that is often on her lips: "I want to do more for Jesus!"

Circle Five: Serving the World

When Jesus called his followers to be a witness for him, he sent us right where we live, all the way to the ends of the earth.[15] This means that serving in our homes, neighborhoods, and community are all essential. But we can't forget to bring the heart and hands of Jesus to the far-flung places of the world.

By God's grace and through the wonderful service of so many people, there are numerous organizations that provide food, clothing, education, and spiritual training for needy people all over the globe.[16] Every family who lives in a part of the world that eats three meals a day and has a safe place to live should pray about partnering with one of these organizations and sponsoring a child or a family. It is a simple way to offer loving service to those in need. In addition, we can partner with our local church or a mission group to participate in service opportunities that bring the love and message of Jesus to our world.

Through giving, praying, going, and supporting existing missions and ministries, we can bring Christ-honoring acts of service to the farthest corners of the globe. Again, no one can tell us exactly what that service should look like. But in each of our personal service portfolios, there should be some investment in the world beyond our local community.

A Vision of Reckless Service

I did not grow up in the church. I became a believer in the middle of the tumultuous season of my teenage years. I lived in Orange County, California, and was engrafted into a wonderful community church in the city of Garden Grove. On Sunday evenings, some of us would go to a powerful worship service at a new church called the Vineyard. They met in the Canyon High School gym.

One Sunday evening, during the singing of a worship song, I had an amazing experience—unlike anything I have had before or since. As I sat on the hard wooden basketball risers, head bowed in prayer, it happened. On the screen of my mind, a scene played out. I could see myself sitting in the gym and Jesus came near me. I could see him. I knew it was Jesus. And . . . he washed my feet.

I know, this might seem far-fetched and strange to you. I know it was to me.

It was just a picture in my mind, some might call it a vision; it seemed real to me as I watched it play out in my mind. In my heart, I knew Jesus was speaking to me. He wanted me to know that if I had been at that table at that last supper over two thousand years before, he would have washed my feet. He washed the feet of a denier, a betrayer, a doubter, and a ragtag bunch of disciples. He would have washed my feet too.

Then, quietly, in my heart, he told me that *he had* washed my feet, more times than I could know. Ultimately, when he died on the cross, he had served me as recklessly as anyone could serve.

I don't know how to put what happened next into words except to say, I was broken. Something deep in my soul shattered. I wept in a way I have done few times in my life. I felt what it was like to have the eternal God of glory, the Lord of the universe, kneel at my feet and wash them. I was undone!

This awareness that Jesus loves me so much that he would recklessly serve a sinner like me changed me. In little ways and big ways, I would never be the same.

Little Steps of Recklessness

Sometimes the littlest things have the biggest impact on us. I call these Seismic Shifts.[17] They are the little things that have a BIG impact on our lives. If you are ready to begin growing in reckless service, start with something simple and small and give it a try. With time, this will form a lifestyle of serving that will have a big impact on all of the people God places in your life.

Here is one little example. Before I understood how Jesus served me and before I heard his call to reckless service, I was famous for calling "Shotgun!" every time I was near a car. I had a unique ability to get the front seat when riding with friends or family members in almost any car.

After that day in the Canyon High School gym when I came to understand that Jesus had washed my feet and called me to wash the feet of others, I decided I would always voluntarily ride in the back and give others the front seat. It was a minuscule thing, but three and a half decades later, it is something I still do. It is a reminder that I am called to humble service and not self-seeking behavior.

Today I serve as the lead pastor of a wonderful church. I see one of my primary roles as serving the pastoral team, directors, and board members. I am called to lead, and I take that very seriously. But first, I am called to serve those I lead. In addition, I am called to teach our pastors to model humble service.

Every Sunday our pastors and leaders drive past the church and down the street. We never seem to have enough parking spots for all those who attend the worship services, so rain or shine, our leaders take the worst spots and walk the longest distance to the church. We don't save the best spots for pastors and put their name on a private parking area. Instead, we invite them to model service by parking the farthest from the church. I think the Bible has something to say about that.[18]

Reflections on Responsible Recklessness

As we serve in our homes, neighborhoods, community, and world, one thing that will become immediately apparent is that the needs around us are enormous. The more we serve, the more needs we will see. If we mail out a check to support a child or family in another part of the world, we just might find three or four more requests in our mailbox the next month. When neighbors see your open door and heart, many will gladly receive the service you offer.

What do we do if the needs become too much for us? How do we respond if people begin making unfair demands on us because they know we love to serve? How do we live a healthy life and not become overwhelmed by the reality of the endless needs all around us?

The answer is, we need to be responsibly reckless. When a need comes our way, we must pray, "God, you love this person more than I do. You can meet every need. Is this specific need one you want to meet through me and the resources you have placed in my care?" Here are two core realities that will help us serve recklessly but also responsibly:

1. A need does not necessitate a call.
2. I can't meet every need—only God can.

Just because we see a need, we are not necessarily called to meet that need. God might have someone else ready to fulfill a particular need. Our job is to be compassionate, available, and responsive to every need God wants us to meet. Always say yes when God calls you to serve. Don't say yes if God is not calling you. This is why prayer is the first part of the Responsible Recklessness Matrix.

Next, apply the second principle of the matrix: gain perspective from the Bible and people you respect. The Bible calls us to reckless service, but it does not teach that you are responsible to meet every need that crosses the radar of your life. Ask people you love and respect if they think you are overextended in service. They will tell you.

Third: be patient and look for the red or green light.

As followers of Jesus, we are wise to serve with joy, passion, and recklessness in a few places and do it well. Some followers of Jesus say yes to every need they encounter, and as a result, they become bitter, resentful, burned out, and sometimes give up on serving altogether.

There is an insightful little cartoon that shows hundreds of faces in a crowd. Each person has a little bubble over their head saying, "What can one person do?" The point of the cartoon is that so many do nothing at all because they are overwhelmed by the massive needs of the world and feel one person can't really make a difference.

How should we respond to the question, "What can one person do?"

We should say, "One person can do a lot. They can do their part." One person can serve, love, and care right where they are in their home, neighborhood, community, and world. But one person can't do everything. We should not try to or pretend we can. We do our part to humbly serve and wash feet like Jesus did. We serve as God leads us, and trust that he will take care of the rest.

Diving into Reckless Service

》 **Praying Reckless Prayers**

Spend time on your own, or with other Christians, and pray in some of the following directions:

- Thank God for his reckless service to you in sending his only Son to this world to live and die for your sins.
- Ask God to help you identify service opportunities he is providing for you in your home, neighborhood, workplace, school, and around the world. Let him know that you will respond and serve, if he will give you a clear leading and a call to action.
- Confess the times you have felt a clear prompting and heard a divine whisper calling you to serve, but you walked past the opportunity.
- Confess where you have overserved and allowed needs to dictate your service rather than actually praying and following God's leading.
- Commit to wash feet in any and every way God calls you to serve and pray for a joyful and humble heart as you embrace these opportunities.

》 **Taking Reckless Actions**

Identify and pray about a specific way you could serve in one or more of the following circles:

    In your home
    In your neighborhood
    In your workplace or school
    In your community
    Around the world

Pray, get perspective (from the Bible and people whom you trust), and be patient as you seek the Lord and ask him to help you identify the specific ways you should be serving.

≫ Thinking Reckless Thoughts

Reflect on some of these questions in the coming days:

- Do I tend to serve others naturally, or do I tend to look for ways that they can serve me?
- How has Jesus served me? What are ways my life reflects the servant heart of my Savior?
- When are the situations, and what are the times, that I tend to think mostly of myself and miss opportunities for reckless service?
- Jesus washed the feet of one who would deny him, one who would doubt him, one who would betray him, and many who would abandon him in his moment of need. If I had been at that table, how would I have felt and responded when Jesus came to wash my feet?
- Which of the disciples' responses have I had toward Jesus at some point in time? How does it change me, realizing that he would have still washed my feet even though he knew I would doubt or deny him?
- How can I live with a greater awareness that I have been mightily served by God?

6

reckless relationships

Some people call me a prop preacher.

During many of my sermons I use a visual of some sort when I seek to communicate the amazing truth of God's Word.

One Sunday morning I began the message standing on a little kid's bed, wearing bright blue pajamas with yellow duckies on them. My message was about how Christians need to learn that, while those scary creatures under our beds are not real, there is one very real monster that lurks in the dark places, waiting to overtake us—the money monster. Money can take on a monster-like role in our life.[1] If we are not on our guard, the money monster will roar his terrible roar, roll his terrible eyes, gnash his terrible teeth, and seek to destroy us![2]

Another time I preached a whole series from the book of Proverbs. We looked at the wrestling match we face every day as the battle between wisdom and folly rages in our soul. I actually preached from a wrestling ring we set up in the middle of the worship center. Everyone remembers the lessons they learned about fighting against folly and living in wisdom during that four-week series.

Sometimes the props I use are subtler. One Sunday we gave each worshiper a packet of honey as they entered the worship center. I was preaching on the doctrine of Scripture, and I had everyone open their honey packet and taste it as I talked about how the Word of God can be as sweet as honey.[3] Another time I held onto two ropes and had church members come up on the platform and pull the ropes in opposite directions. We were studying the doctrine of the Trinity. As these two people tried to pull me in opposite directions, I talked about the dynamic theological tension that comes when we seek to hold onto two beliefs that seem to be in opposition to each other. In the case of the Trinity, Christians hold on to the truth that God is Father, Son, and Holy Spirit, revealing himself as three distinct persons.[4] At the same time, he is not three gods, but one God.[5] As I preached, we hung a sign on one rope that said "God is Trinity." On the other rope was a sign that said "God is One." As my two helpers pulled on their ropes and stretched my arms outward, I talked about how we must hold on to both of these clear teachings of the Bible. Even when it is difficult to fully understand the mystery of the Trinity, we can't let go of either of these teachings. If we did, we would compromise the orthodox and true faith taught in the Bible.

In a sermon series about biblical relationships, I illustrated my point with a simple, yet powerful, picture of a human chain. I invited Howie Hugo, the founding pastor of Shoreline Church, to stand at the top of the platform. Howie is still on the staff team at the church and I meet with him regularly to learn from his wisdom, ask questions about ministry, and draw from his experience leading the church for fifteen years before he passed the baton to me.

Next, I stood on the middle stair that goes up to the platform, and held Howie's hand. I talked about how I need people in my life who are farther down the road of faith and leadership and who can help me grow and move forward. I told the congregation about how I love to spend time with Howie, receive his encouragement, and learn from him.[6]

Then, I invited Jonathan Ryan, a young man in our congregation, to come and stand on the bottom of the stairs. He and I also held hands. I talked about what a joy it is to invest time, prayer, and hopefully some of the wisdom I have gained into the next generation. Jonathan is our worship leader and we work closely together. I have opportunity, on a regular basis, to invest in his life and faith. (As a matter of fact, I had the privilege of performing his wedding a short time before I finished writing this book.)

There we stood, a picture of three generations of faith. Our hands locked together to portray the importance of relationships and to symbolize how we need each other.

Do you get the picture? It is a beautiful one.

We can't walk through life alone. As followers of Christ we should have people who are farther up the road of faith holding our hand and helping us along. At the same time, we each need to let God use us to help others along. This kind of connection and community should be normative for followers of Jesus.

Picture yourself on your journey of faith. Who is ahead of you, helping you forward? Whose hand are you holding as you help them grow in faith and spiritual maturity?

Nothing Matters More!

There is nothing more significant than loving relationships. In the entire universe, nothing trumps their value and importance.

Jesus made this clear when he taught that the greatest of all the commandments is to love God. The second is similar. We are to love others.[7] Of the hundreds of commandments recorded in Scripture, Jesus distilled things down to this simple but challenging reality. Nothing compares to the importance of building loving and healthy relationships.

First and foremost we are to invest in our friendship with God. Then, close on the heels of this commitment is the value and primacy of how we relate to others. Since we looked at the topic of loving God in chapter 3, we will devote this chapter to the topic of building loving relationships with other people.

God himself exists in eternal and perfect community.[8] We use the term *Trinity* to express the mysterious reality that God exists as three distinct persons, yet he is one God. The Athanasian Creed describes the Trinity this way:

> We worship one God in trinity and the trinity in
>   unity,
> neither blending their persons
> nor dividing their essence.
>
> For the person of the Father is a distinct person,
> the person of the Son is another,
> and that of the Holy Spirit still another.
> But the divinity of the Father, Son, and Holy Spirit is
>   one,
> their glory equal, their majesty coeternal.
>
> What quality the Father has, the Son has, and the
>   Holy Spirit has.
> The Father is uncreated,
> the Son is uncreated,
> the Holy Spirit is uncreated.
>
> The Father is immeasurable,
> the Son is immeasurable,
> the Holy Spirit is immeasurable.
>
> The Father is eternal,
> the Son is eternal,
> the Holy Spirit is eternal.
>
> And yet there are not three eternal beings;
> there is but one eternal being.[9]

Since God models perfect community and Jesus calls us to loving relationships, we should be highly committed to locking arms with each other and building the kind of relationships that honor God. Each of us should look closely at what it will take for us to grow reckless in our relationships, for the sake of Jesus.

Relationships with God's People

Over the past three decades I have been warmly embraced in the Church, God's family. Having grown up with virtually no spiritual connections or Christian faith, I feel like an adopted son in the local church. I have experienced the privilege of spending time with Christians in many parts of the world and have been consistently struck with the same observations and feelings.

I like these people!

Most Christians I meet are kind, generous, and seeking to follow Jesus. Believers around the world, and right where I live, really love God and want to honor him. They desire to be part of a loving and healthy Christian community. They long to share the love and message of Jesus with those who have not yet entered a life-saving relationship with God.

As a brand-new Christian, I attended a church with over 10,000 members and a youth ministry with over 1,000 students. In this mass of people, a number of Christians reached out to me before I embraced Jesus, and they continued to invest in me after I became a Christ follower. Dan, the ministry leader, spoke at youth group almost every week. Among all the other students, he knew who I was and even challenged me to develop my teaching gift at a young age. Glenn and Doug were volunteer leaders who went to college full-time but also helped high school kids like me learn about God and the Bible. They cheered me on as I took my first steps of faith and challenged me to keep growing once I received Jesus.

When I moved away from California to attend a Christian college in Wheaton, Illinois, a couple named Mark and Cindy reached out to me and took me under their wing. They invited me to serve in a high school ministry and embraced me in their family. It made my time at college so much better.

In the first church that I served as a pastor, a delightful woman named Twila adopted me, Sherry, and our firstborn son, Zach. She was a retired neonatal nurse and offered to babysit some evenings while we were engaged in church ministry. For almost two decades after I left that church, Twila still prayed for us and sent a yearly Christmas letter and update. She became family.

I could go on for the rest of this book and write about people in the churches we have served, including Jay and Lucille, who showered us with support and prayers from the day we met; Warren, who mentored and encouraged me for many years; Chuck and Jean, who have invested wisdom and care in Sherry and me for over two decades; and more people than I can number. For the most part, folks in the local church have reflected the beauty and grace of Jesus to my family and me. This continues into the present in the church I serve. The people at Shoreline Church are caring, kind, and seeking to bring the light of Jesus to our community.

Okay, I admit it. I am a huge fan of Christians and the local church.

I love the picture the apostle Paul paints of the early believers:

> They devoted themselves to the apostles' teaching and to the fellowship, to the breaking of bread and to prayer. Everyone was filled with awe, and many wonders and miraculous signs were done by the apostles. All the believers were together and had everything in common. Selling their possessions and goods, they gave to anyone as he had need. Every day they continued to meet together in the temple courts. They broke bread in their homes and ate together with glad and sincere hearts, praising God and enjoying the favor of all the

people. And the Lord added to their number daily those who were being saved. (Acts 2:42–47)

What a hope-filled vision! The church was a body of people who gathered in corporate settings for worship as well as informally in homes. They were committed to learning and feeding on God's Word and sharing in fellowship. They gave sacrificially to each other and met monetary needs as they arose. The believers in Jesus were sincere and joyful, and their presence in the world made a difference. Spiritually curious people came to faith in the Savior because of the example, lives, and testimonies of these people.

The early Christians functioned as a body. Every member was needed and valued. The apostle Paul painted a vivid picture of church members being closely connected with the integration of a physical body.[10] We are to have such organic connection to each other that it is almost impossible for us to function alone. We all know that if a hand or foot is amputated, it is lifeless. In Paul's mind, this is a picture of a Christian who is not connected in a local Christian community. Disconnection means death.

The author of the book of Hebrews raises this same concern by saying, "Let us not give up meeting together, as some are in the habit of doing, but let us encourage one another—and all the more as you see the Day approaching."[11] Followers of Jesus are called to reckless relationships where we share, love, care, support, challenge, and walk through life together.

This is an important corrective for some Christians today. Too many believers feel they can live in spiritual isolation from the broader church. Maybe you have heard declarations like these:

"I don't really go to church, I meet God in nature!"
"I have been hurt by people in the church. I am fine reading my Bible at home and watching an occasional service

online or on television. I have no need or desire to attend a church service."

"I have been in the church and those people are a bunch of hypocrites. I have no interest in being around people like that."

"I don't believe in the whole modern church thing. God has never been about big groups gathering in massive worship centers. His vision is small clusters in home groups."

"Church is inconvenient for me. It just does not fit in my schedule. I am fine meeting God wherever I am."

I am sure you could add more examples to this list, but you get the point. There are a lot of people who lean toward an isolated faith where they are not gathering with older people who can take their hand and help them forward. They are also not investing in the next generation and helping others along. They stand alone and there is no one to help when they fall.

In the book of Ecclesiastes we read,

> Two are better than one,
> because they have a good return for their work:
> If one falls down,
>   his friend can help him up.
> But pity the man who falls
>   and has no one to help him up!
> Also, if two lie down together, they will keep warm.
>   But how can one keep warm alone?
> Though one may be overpowered,
>   two can defend themselves.
> A cord of three strands is not quickly broken. (Eccl. 4:9–12)

This passage praises the value of connection and community. The local church is the best place to experience this. We need to gather with people from various age groups, walks of life, backgrounds, and levels of spiritual development. We are all stronger when we lock arms with people who can teach us and help us along. At the same time, we grow healthier in faith as we invest in people who are younger in their walk with Jesus. These people need us to cheer them on and support them in their adventure of faith. Together, we can become reckless and bold as we walk with Jesus.

When I read the words "A cord of three strands is not quickly broken," I picture Howie Hugo holding one of my hands and helping me in my life and ministry. I see Jonathan Ryan locked on my other arm and God using me to help him forward. This kind of partnership is not quickly broken, and it leads to strength, courage, and reckless faith, because we are never alone. If we fall, and we all do, there are people to pick us up and help us along.

People isolate themselves for many reasons, and some are not necessarily unfounded. Although most people in the church are kind and gracious, there are some tough people wandering the halls of local congregations. There are hypocrites in the church. People who claim to love Jesus can hurt each other deeply. Establishing a rhythm of attending a worship service every week can be difficult because of a work schedule. Or it can simply be inconvenient. Being in a small group for learning, accountability, and fellowship can be challenging and stretch us, especially if we are more introverted by nature. But God designed us for community and calls us to reckless relationships with other Christians . . . even when it is difficult!

If we engage with the Christians in our local church and those in other congregations, it will mean time, effort, and reckless trust in God. These people could hurt us. They might let us down. We might even end up being the one who brings pain to the life of another believer. But the astonishing benefits of being in community with other Christ followers will outweigh the risks, if we dare to recklessly trust God. When we do, he can do a deeper work in and through us than we would ever experience apart from the body of Christ.

Some years ago a publisher asked Sherry and me to write a book about finding the right church. The idea was to write a simple little book that could be a road map for those looking for a home church. The working title they suggested was *Finding a Church You Can Love.* We were excited about the concept but had one serious reservation. It felt like the goal of this book was self-centered. It was all about finding a church that fit us.

Sherry and I agreed to write the book with one condition. We wanted to change the title to *Finding a Church You Can Love, and Loving the Church You've Found.*[12] We insisted that there be a second section in the book that would help people discover how they could serve, connect, and give back to the body of Christ. If we are part of a church and only think about what we can gain, we become consumers of religious goods. When we discover that the church creates a place where we can receive and give to others, we learn the joy of Christian community.

If you want to experience a life of reckless faith, get into a local church and learn to love it. Don't just ask, "What does this church have to offer me?" but invest in the lives of others. Find a place to serve. Welcome new visitors. Help those who are new in faith grow deeper. Get in a small group and build relationships. Volunteer in areas of ministry that fit your spiritual gifts. Make friends. Worship God with passion. And discover the joy of being part of God's gathered family.

Relationships with People Who Are Not Followers of Jesus

Christian community and being part of a local church are essential for a healthy life of faith. God delights when we are active in the body of Christ, his family. But too many Christians get so invested in relationships with their believing friends that they forget to develop and nurture friendships with those who have not come to experience and embrace the grace of Jesus.

It is easy to circle the spiritual wagons and take a defensive attitude toward the world. Some Christians see nonbelievers as the enemy. When this attitude prevails, we tend to break off our relationships with people who are not Christians. If we do interact with nonbelievers, we tend to keep these relationships shallow and safe.

This way of thinking is diametrically opposed to the example of Jesus. It is contrary to the very heartbeat of God. Think about it—God left the glory of heaven to come and live among people who hated him and would one day kill him.[13] While we were sinful and rebellious, Jesus entered our world to give his life for us.[14] God loved the people of the world so much that he offered his beloved Son as the sacrifice for our sins.[15] The story of Christmas is the perfect example of God's commitment to enter relationship with the people who needed him.

When Jesus walked on this earth, he did not cloister himself in a religious community and avoid the irreligious people of his day. On the contrary, Jesus loved to hang out with sinners, prostitutes, tax collectors, lepers, and outcasts.[16] These people, who were ostracized from the religious community, were drawn to Jesus. In the Gospels we learn that Jesus was so comfortable with the irreligious and broken of his day that some of the "religious elite" were offended and bothered.[17]

When was the last time you were accused of being a "friend of tax collectors and sinners"? Jesus had this label slapped on him, and he wore it with delight. So should we. As followers of Jesus, we are to live as he lived, love as he loved, go where he went. Ultimately we should reflect the teachings and example of Jesus.

If you are a follower of Jesus who spends little or no time with people who are spiritually disconnected from God, it may be time to be reckless, make some new friends, and spend consistent time with them. If you are at church during all of your free time, you should evaluate your priorities. If you say, "I really don't have any close friends who are nonbelievers," God has a message for you.

He wants to bring love, grace, and the good news of his Son to our world, and you are called to be part of this mission. You are God's light on this dark planet. You are the salt that God wants to use to cause people to thirst for the living water that only Jesus can provide.[18] God wants to work in and through you to share his love naturally with others through organic outreach.[19] This can only happen when you are in close proximity to people who need Jesus. It happens as you establish authentic and loving relationships with people outside your church.

Bridging Your Worlds

You might be thinking, which is it? First you write about the importance of spending time with Christians and being an active and investing member of a local church. Then you emphasize the critical importance of having authentic and deep friendships with nonbelievers and you say, "Spend less time with Christians and don't get overcommitted at church."

You might be thinking, make up your mind—should we invest heavily in the church community or in the people who are still far from God?

The answer is, both! This is not an either/or proposition.

God expects us to commit ourselves to both of these with great passion. Some people reading this book need to work on developing relationships with other Christians and connecting in a local congregation. If this is you, you might need to find a church, get in a small group, and go deeper with your brothers and sisters in Christ. Most of your time is spent connecting with people who are not believers and you need to grow closer ties with other Christians . . . but still keep vibrant friendships with the spiritually disconnected. Your reckless move is to open your heart to the people in a local fellowship and go deeper with Christians.

Others are overinvested in the church and should leverage more time in their friendship with spiritual seekers. If this is you, it might be time to take up a hobby where you can meet some new people in your community. Maybe you need to contact a nonbelieving acquaintance you have not spent time with for quite a while. The truth is, you have a long list of Christian friends you love, but God is calling you to spend less time at church and more time in the world. Your reckless move is establishing a balanced rhythm in your life that affords good time with people who still need to experience the amazing grace and love of Jesus.

When we are committed to nurture healthy community with other Christians and build strong friendships with spiritual seekers, the fun really begins. This is when things can get reckless, exciting, and transformational. When this happens, you can begin to build intentional bridges between these two relational worlds. Sadly, many Christians keep these worlds separate. They have a circle of Christian friends who only hang out with other believers. They also have a group of nonbelieving friends from work or some social setting, but these two worlds are like islands. They seem so far apart. What God wants us to do is bridge these worlds and bring people together.

In the Gospels we meet a man named Matthew.[20] He was a tax collector. In his day this meant he was a traitor to his people, cast out of the religious and social circles of those who followed God. His circle of friends were thieves, tax collectors, prostitutes, and sinners. When Jesus met Matthew, he could see past the outer crust to a heart that was soft and ready to enter a relationship with the Savior. Once Matthew became a follower of Jesus, he naturally became a bridge between his two relational worlds.

Matthew had his new friends, Jesus and the disciples. He also had his old friends, a bunch of tax collectors and sinners.

Matthew brought them all together at a big party.[21] What a great picture! He did not keep these worlds separate but integrated them. Matthew was a bridge builder. This kind of relational connecting is reckless and powerful. It should be normative in the life of every follower of Jesus.

In your personal life, look for natural opportunities to connect your Christian friends with those who do not yet know Jesus. Have a party and invite friends from both worlds. When you are going to an appropriate church gathering, invite a friend who is open spiritually. If you are part of a social gathering with nonchurched people, see if one of your Christian friends can come along. Make it your mission to be a bridge builder.

In your church, set a goal to have regular events that non-believers would enjoy. Be aggressively intentional about having church members invite spiritually disconnected people to these gatherings. At one church where I served, a group of couples met every month to play a card game called euchre. Ten to twenty couples would meet in homes, not on the church campus. They had a blast! One of the great things about these evenings was that people could invite nonchurched friends to come, hang out, play, and have fun. It was a nonthreatening and natural way to connect their worlds. At Shoreline Church we hold occasional "Open Mic Nights." These are evenings with great refreshments, warm people, and a stage with an open mic. It is always fun to see what the various artists from the church and the community bring as they share the stage, read original poetry, perform music—they have fun and get to know each other. This builds all sorts of wonderful bridges.

You get the picture. God wants us to have strong relationships with Christians. We need to be connected in the church. We should also have rich and growing friendships with people in our community who do not yet know the love and grace of Jesus. We are to let God's light shine through us in our world. Finally, we should joyfully construct bridges between these two worlds so God can use us to bring his message of grace to the world.

Reflections on Reckless Relationships

Christians are called to love the lost, pray for the world, be salt and light, and witness to those who are still far from Jesus. We are also warned that we are not to be conformed to this world.[22] We are to be reckless as we engage in authentic and deep friendships with people who are far from Jesus and living deep in sin. But we also need to be responsible. We pray, we gain perspective, and we are patient as we determine where our lives should intersect in the world.

If a new believer has come out of drug addiction and alcoholism, they might need to avoid certain people and places that present too great a temptation . . . at least for a time. We are called to be reckless, but God does not want us to spiral back into a life of sin and rebellion. Even those of us who have been Christ followers for a while should be wary of going where the temptation is simply too great for us to handle. Before you jump into a worldly setting that is filled with potential pitfalls and temptations, walk through the Responsible Recklessness Matrix:

Pray . . . God, is this a place I can be an influencer and not be enticed into sin and compromise?

Perspective . . . Ask mature believers who know and love you, "Do you think this is a relationship that is healthy for me? Do you think I am ready to enter this place and will be able to bring the light of Jesus with me?"

Patience . . . If you are a new believer, give yourself some time to grow in faith before you move into situations and relationships with nonbelievers that could cause you to stumble.

When Christians build close relationships with nonbelievers and enter secular settings, there are always potential risks. We must be responsible and careful, yet we are also called to reckless relationships. If we can stand strong and resist the temptations inherent in being in the world, we should boldly and recklessly enter in and become bridge builders for the glory of Jesus.

Diving into Reckless Relationships

>> **Praying Reckless Prayers**

Spend time on your own, or with other Christians, and pray in some of the following directions:

- Thank God for the people in your life right now who have taken your hand and are helping you grow and move forward in your walk with Jesus.
- Ask God to use you to help others grow in faith. Pray that others will be strengthened as you take their hand and help them on their journey of faith.
- Praise God, the Trinity, for existing in eternal and perfect community. Celebrate how God is moving in your life as Father, Son, and Holy Spirit.
- Invite God to move you forward into deeper connections in both the church and the world.
- Pray for courage to be a bridge builder. Ask God to guide you as you seek to connect your Christian friends and your nonbelieving friends.

>> **Taking Reckless Actions**

Plan a Matthew party. Make time in the coming week to bring some Christian friends together with some non-Christian friends. Make sure it is in a safe and inviting environment. You might even want to consider doing this with your small group members.

>> **Thinking Reckless Thoughts**

Reflect on some of these questions in the coming days:

- What are some ways I can deepen and strengthen my relationships with other followers of Jesus?
- How can I develop new and stronger friendships with people who are not yet believers in Jesus?
- What can I learn from God's eternal community of Father, Son, and Holy Spirit?

- Who, among the people I know, naturally build bridges between Christians and those who are not yet followers of Jesus? What can I learn from their example?
- Who are nonbelievers I know whom I have not connected with for a long time? How can I reengage in my relationships with these people?

7

reckless prayers

Jesus lifted up one of the most reckless prayers in the history of the world. When he was on the Mount of Olives, as the cross was looming in his future, Jesus prayed these words: "Not my will, but yours be done."[1] This is the prayer of a yielded heart. Jesus, God in human flesh, surrendered his life to the will of the Father. This kind of prayer becomes a launchpad for reckless, adventurous, world-changing action.

Jesus was not giving some hypothetical nod of the head as if to say, "I am asking the Father to place a divine rubber stamp on my desires." On the contrary, Jesus knew what was on the horizon: rejection by his friends, ridicule from the religious community, lies and false accusations, judgment for all human sin, the torment of the cross, and ultimately the wrath of the Father descending on him with such crushing force that it would kill him.

When Jesus declared, "Your will be done," it was not lip service or religious jargon. It was absolute and reckless surrender to the will of the Father . . . no matter what the cost.

These four words just might be the most reckless prayer anyone could ever lift up—YOUR WILL BE DONE!

Jesus calls us to reckless faith that includes this kind of prayer. He modeled it for us and ended up nailed to a Roman cross, bearing the sins of the very people who mocked, beat, and hated him.

Your Will Be Done!

Jesus taught his followers to pray something very similar. In what we call "The Lord's Prayer," Jesus taught us to pray, "Your kingdom come, your will be done, on earth as it is in heaven."[2] There it is again, those four radical and life-changing words, "Your will be done." In addition, Jesus calls us to surrender to the establishment of God's kingdom on this earth, in our culture, church, workplace, neighborhood, home, and heart.

Before we begin lifting up reckless prayers as an expression of our faith, it is essential to realize that these prayers are almost always about surrendering to God's will, design, and vision of his glorious kingdom.

Too often our approach to prayer is about deciding what we want, what we like, what would bring us the greatest joy, and asking God to sign on the dotted line. When God does what we ask, we are thankful. If God fails to deliver and perform as we request, we end up disappointed or even upset with him.

Some will go so far as to walk away from faith in God because he did not say, "How high?" when they said, "Jump." In its grossest form there are those who codify a whole system of theology that says prayer is really about us claiming what we want and praying in such a way that God has *no option* but to perform and deliver as we demand. These hucksters of religious trinkets and false promises do great damage to people who buy into this false teaching. They end up being disappointed by a mirage of a "god" invented by confused people seeking to satisfy their own desires. Sadly, these people never meet the real Maker of heaven and earth because they are chasing after a deity of their own design.

At other times we talk to God about what we don't like, the things we do not enjoy, and we tell God that we would like to have him protect us from anything that brings pain and inconvenience to our lives. In short, prayer becomes our tool to protect us from hurt, struggle, or suffering. When we are in a good patch on the road, we can be grateful. When there are potholes and the going is rough, we wonder why God did not protect us.

Reckless prayer, as modeled and taught by Jesus, is about surrender to the will of God. It is focused on asking for his kingdom—not our own—to come. It is about rejoicing in his will, even when it is hard and costs us greatly. Reckless prayer is counterintuitive and utterly selfless.

Your kingdom!
Your will!
Your glory!
Your name be lifted up!

When this vision of prayer grips our heart, the list of demands on God becomes much shorter. The Christmas list of toys and trinkets that we never really needed begins to look childish . . . because it is.

Dangerous and reckless prayer drives us deep into the heart of God and away from our self-motivated whims.

What might tomorrow look like if you began your day with the simple but life-changing prayer, "Your will be done"? What if your driving passion was God's glory and desire expressed in these words, "Thy will be done," and not personal gain and comfort that moves you to cry, "My will be done"?

Grow Your Fruit

As a young believer in Jesus, I learned about the fruit of the Spirit quite early. I had a love/hate relationship with those two very popular verses from the apostle Paul's letter to the Galatian Christians. "But the fruit of the Spirit is love, joy, peace, patience, kindness, goodness, faithfulness, gentleness and self-control. Against such things there is no law."[3] I loved this list of nine qualities that mark the life of a Christian, because I longed to reflect these characteristics in my life. I struggled with these lofty ideals because none of them were developed, in any significant way, in my young life of faith. They reminded me of where I was heading, but also of how far I had to go.

For many years I prayed, "Grow your fruit in me, dear Lord!" I invited the Holy Spirit to mature me, convict me, and change me. As a young believer I was deeply touched by an old praise chorus that had a simple tune, but reckless words:

> Spirit of the living God, fall afresh on me;
> Spirit of the living God, fall afresh on me.
> Melt me, mold me, fill me, use me.
> Spirit of the Living God, fall afresh on me.[4]

Early in my faith, this prayer, set to music, became a heartfelt invitation for the Spirit to move and do whatever he wanted in me. In my prayer life I would identify one fruit of the Spirit that was lacking and would cry out for God to grow this in me. These prayers, over many years, led to both painful and glorious moments of transformation.

God did not answer my prayer for patience by magically making me more patient while I slept at night. Instead, he put tough situations in my life that became the fire in which the Spirit could forge a patient heart and attitude deep within me. The Spirit of God lovingly directed me toward people who drove me crazy, and the consistent proximity forced me to increase in patience. I wish I could tell you that when I prayed for a specific fruit to grow, it happened with no challenge or pain, but that would be a lie. Each time I spent a season praying for a particular fruit of the Spirit to grow (and some of these seasons of prayer would last for months), God would bring experiences, people, and challenges that would become the fertile soil of transformation.

As I prayed for self-control, it seemed the things that would trigger self-indulgence and sinful hedonism would come at me more often and with greater force. This drove me to pray, examine my life, and cry to God for help. It matured me. And with time, self-control began to blossom.

I have been praying, "Lord, grow your fruit in me," for over three decades. I am still a work in progress. God, in his grace, is answering this reckless prayer with each passing day. For the record, it is still a hard process, but a glorious one!

About twenty years ago this prayer began to take new shape in my life. My wife, Sherry, and I have three sons, and they were about one, three, and five years old at the time. I looked at these precious little boys and wanted to see them grow to be men who loved God, followed Jesus, and exhibited the fruit of the Spirit in profound ways.

Before they had any idea what I was doing, I began to pray the fruit of the Spirit for my children. I did this knowing the process of growing these characteristics and traits is never easy and often painful. I had a clear awareness that if God answered my prayer, it would most certainly lead to times of painful refining in each of their lives.

I would wait on the Lord quietly and ask, for each son, what fruit does he need to have grow and blossom in his life right now? Sometimes the answer would come right away . . . it was obvious. At other times I would pray for days before I had a clear direction about which fruit of the Spirit I was to pray for. Over the last twenty years I have cried out to God on behalf of my sons. I have prayed the various fruits of the Spirit for each of them. The results have been glorious.

I remember a time God prompted me to pray for joy to grow in the heart and life of one of my boys. I prayed for this fruit for almost two years. I never told him that God had whispered to me to intercede and pray for this fruit. Over the months, I saw it grow. Slowly, almost imperceptibly at first. I watched God break things in my son that needed to be dealt with. I saw spiritual discipline come from the loving hands of God. Over time an authentic and Spirit-given joy began to change my son's attitudes, countenance, and relationships.

I have lost count of the number of times I have secretly prayed for a fruit of the Spirit to grow in the life of one of my sons and seen a noticeable change in a matter of days or weeks.

Because of the amazing power of this kind of intercession, about ten years ago I began praying, "God, grow your fruit," for my wife, siblings, friends in ministry, and many other Christians I know and care about.

Will you dare to pray for the fruit of the Spirit to grow in your life? Will you get reckless and ask the Holy Spirit of God to grow his fruit in the lives of those you love, even if it means they might have to be refined and go through the furnace? Will you commit to pray for a specific fruit to grow in the life of a believer you love? If you are not sure where to start, invite God to show you. Lift up these reckless words of intercession, "God, grow your fruit!" Do it knowing full well that God might need to till the soil, remove some weeds, and create an environment where the fruit can grow. This is a dangerous, reckless, and glorious way to pray!

Speak, Lord, Your Servant Is Listening

Do you believe God speaks today? Can a follower of Jesus hear divine whispers and learn to follow the leading of the Savior?[5] Do the sheep of God's pasture have the ability to hear and recognize the voice of the Good Shepherd? Jesus seemed to think that this was not only possible, but that it should be normative.

"I tell you the truth, the man who does not enter the sheep pen by the gate, but climbs in by some other way, is a thief and a robber. The man who enters by the gate is the shepherd of his sheep. The watchman opens the gate for him, and the sheep listen to his voice. He calls his own sheep by name and leads them out. When he has brought out all his own, he goes on ahead of them, and his sheep follow him because they know his voice. But they will never follow a stranger; in fact, they will run away from him because they do not recognize a stranger's voice." Jesus used this figure of speech, but they did not understand what he was telling them. (John 10:1–6)

The sheep of Jesus's pasture recognize the voice of their Shepherd. They can differentiate between the Shepherd and a stranger. Jesus clearly teaches his followers that they will recognize his voice. He was also quick to point out that many who listened to him did not get the heart of what he was trying to communicate.

I fear this is still the case today. Far too many Christians do not invite God to speak. We don't slow down, quiet our hearts, and listen for the voice of our heavenly Good Shepherd. Instead, we can let clutter, busyness, or fear get in the way.

If you want to grow reckless in your prayer life, make a commitment to make time and space to say, "Speak, Lord, your servant is listening." Then, actually pay attention and follow the leading of Jesus.

Not growing up in church or learning from the Bible, I had no preconceived notions about prayer. I did not do bedtime prayers. I did not kneel next to my bed at night with folded hands and pray, "Now I lay me down to sleep, I pray the Lord my soul to keep . . ." I never stopped to thank God for a meal. As a fresh, new follower of Jesus, spiritually speaking, I was a blank slate.

What I had learned in the first few months I had been hanging around Christians was that these people talked about God like they knew him. They spoke of Jesus as if he was a close friend. When they prayed, it sounded like they were talking to a real person.

The night I confessed my sins and surrendered my life to follow Jesus, I heard God speak for the first of many times. I was lying on the roof of a houseboat in the Sacrament Delta packed into my sleeping bag. I was looking into the star-pierced sky. I did not really ask God to speak, yet I was not at all surprised when he did. It all felt strangely normal. I did not hear him with my ears, but I recognized his voice. He spoke just one line: "Spend the rest of your life telling people about me or you'll be miserable."

Some people might not like the idea of God telling a young man who just came to faith in Jesus that he would be miserable if he did not invest his life in telling others about the Savior, but it made perfect sense to me. I did not know much at fifteen years old. What I did know was that I did not want to be miserable!

I responded by simply telling God, "Okay."

The next morning I told one of the youth leaders that I wanted to become a pastor and tell others about Jesus. I asked him what I needed to do next. First, he said, "Get a haircut!" He followed that comment with a hearty laugh to assure me that cutting my long blond hair was not a requirement. He got more serious and said, "You will probably need to graduate from high school and maybe do a bit more school after that." He knew I had a 0.75 GPA the previous year and that my interests were split evenly between the beach and girls. He also got me a Bible and told me I should read it . . . which I did.

Within the first few hours of becoming a follower of Jesus, I began listening for God to speak. I believe this should be normative for all Christians. Jesus is the Good Shepherd and we are his sheep. We can learn to recognize his voice, knowing that God will never call us to do anything contrary to the clear teaching of the Bible. The authority of the Scriptures trumps any whisper or prompting that is inconsistent with the teaching of God's Word.

I love the story recorded in 1 Samuel 3. Eli is a prophet of the Lord and he is training and mentoring young Samuel to be a servant of God. One night Samuel hears a voice call out his name. His response is natural and completely un-understandable—he runs to the prophet Eli, assuming he has called him. Eli sends him back to bed, assuring him that he had not. This happens three times in rapid succession. By the third time it hits the elderly Eli . . . God is speaking to Samuel. The aging prophet gives him these instructions, "Go and lie down, and if he calls you, say, 'Speak, LORD, for your servant is listening.'"[6]

The fourth time God calls Samuel's name, he follows Eli's instructions and responds, "Speak, for your servant is listening." This life-changing encounter with God was transformational for Samuel. He began listening to God and never stopped. All through his ministry recorded in the Old Testament, Samuel had open lines of communication with God—as if he and God were in conversation.[7]

For Samuel the journey began with a very specific prayer, "Speak, for your servant is listening." We can and should learn to echo this prayer. You and I can experience dramatic life change and clear leading as we listen for the voice of the Good Shepherd and learn to recognize when he speaks to us. There are many ways God's voice can be heard. The clearest and unchanging way God communicates with us is through the text of the Bible. His Word is always true, and we are wise to read it and seek God's direction for our lives each and every day. It is our measuring stick, and anyone or anything that does not agree with the teaching of Scripture is simply wrong.

In addition to the Bible, God can speak through people, situations, dreams, visions, and by the gentle voice of the Holy Spirit.[8] I wrote a book some years ago in which I looked at the many ways God speaks to his children. In this book I also dig into ways we can increase our ability to hear from God.[9] As the years have passed, I have grown even more convicted that followers of Jesus need to learn to make time and space to be quiet, to listen, to wait on the Lord, and to expect to receive his leading.

This kind of prayer can involve asking God good questions and listening for the voice of the Holy Spirit to answer. The more we speak with God and listen for his responses, the greater chance we have of hearing from him. Here are some questions you might want to use as you seek to listen for the still small voice of God's Spirit:

- How much do you love me, God, and how have you shown your love?
- What attitudes and actions in my life dishonor you and need to stop?
- Is there a person in my life who needs to encounter your love and grace through an act of service I could offer?
- What can I do to help others see your presence alive in me?
- Is there some good habit or spiritual discipline I need to begin and engraft into the rhythm of my life?
- What step can I take today to live more for the glory of Jesus?

Occasionally I meet a sincere and godly Christian who says, "I don't believe God still speaks today. We have the Bible and that is enough." In some cases they are very worried that people will go too far with the whole "listening to God" thing and become irresponsibly reckless.

This is a fair concern. But it should not keep us from following the clear teaching of the Bible. God speaks to his children. His Word teaches this over and over again. We should always be ready to listen and obey his promptings, whispers, and directives.

If you are ready to engage in reckless prayer, invite God to speak to you. Be quiet and listen. Follow God's leading in your life. If the whisper is from God, it will always be consistent with the teaching of the Bible. As you learn to listen to God's voice, you will, with ever-increasing clarity, recognize the voice of your Good Shepherd.

Open Our Eyes So We Can See

God is present. He is alive, moving, and active in our world, far more than most of us recognize. If we live with eyes open to see the presence of God, we will grow powerfully confident and recklessly adventurous. The many limitations we put on ourselves will begin to melt away when we see that we are not alone, but powerfully supported by the presence of Jesus. This should not surprise us. Jesus promised he would be with us always.[10]

This spiritual reality is painted with bold and graphic strokes in the story of Elisha and his servant.[11] Elisha, the prophet of God, had been involved in insider trading. God was telling him all the plans and military strategies of the king of Aram. Every time this king plotted an attack on the people of Israel, God would tell Elisha and Elisha would tell the king of Israel. This infuriated the king of Aram, who assumed that one of his own men must have been a double agent selling information to his enemies.

When the king of Aram learned the truth and discovered that Elisha was telling the king of Israel all of his plans to conquer cities on Israel's borders, he decided to capture and kill the blabbermouth prophet. He found out where he was staying and surrounded the city in the middle of the night. Watch closely what happens next:

> When the servant of the man of God got up and went out early the next morning, an army with horses and chariots had surrounded the city. "Oh, my lord, what shall we do?" the servant asked.

"Don't be afraid," the prophet answered. "Those who are with us are more than those who are with them."

And Elisha prayed, "O LORD, open his eyes so he may see." Then the LORD opened the servant's eyes, and he looked and saw the hills full of horses and chariots of fire all around Elisha. (2 Kings 6:15–17)

Can you imagine the *fear* of Elisha's servant when he went out of the city in the morning and saw the army of the Arameans surrounding the city? He must have thought, "We're dead now. There is no way out of this!"

Can you imagine the *frustration* of Elisha's servant when he looked at the prophet acting so calm, confident, and cool in the face of a massive army surrounding him? He must have thought, "What is wrong with Elijah? Doesn't he realize we are trapped like rats?"

Can you imagine the *faith* that filled Elisha's servant when his eyes were opened and he saw the hills covered with horses and chariots of fire around Elisha? He must have thought, "No wonder Elisha is always so faith-filled—he has a personal heavenly bodyguard all around him . . . and he knows it!"

Elisha had an extraordinary level of faith, but he also had eyes to see the spiritual realities around him. He was profoundly aware of God's presence and sovereign power. He could speak with reckless boldness and walk with stunning confidence, because he saw the presence of God, the angelic warriors around him, and the continual evidence of God's saving power in his life.

What would happen if you began to pray, "Open my eyes so I can see"? Would you be more spiritually confident and take a few more chances if you were deeply convinced that God is on the throne, his angels are around you, and he can win any victory he wants to win? Do you dare to ask God to open your eyes to his presence, power, and authority in this sin-torn world?

What might happen if you began praying for other Christians around you to have their eyes opened to the reality of

God's presence—even in the tough times? All through the Bible, God showed power and glory to his people. Daniel was protected by angels when he was tossed into the lions' den.[12] In the year that King Uzziah died and the nation was filled with fear at the coming political turmoil, Isaiah saw the Lord high and lifted up![13] When John was in prison on the island of Patmos in a time of horrific persecution of the church and when Christians were being martyred for faith in Jesus, he saw a vision of Jesus in absolute glory and victory.[14] Over and over the people of God were allowed to see a hope-filled spiritual reality when everything on the outside seemed lost.

If Christians today could get a glimpse behind the veil of eternity, we would be amazed to see that the Lord of Glory is still on the throne, all the resources of the universe are at his disposal, and he can send a delegation of angelic warriors to protect his people and accomplish his will at any moment.

If we respond like Elisha's servant did at first glance and look only at the enemy army surrounding us, we will be paralyzed and ineffective. If we ask God to open our eyes, and the eyes of other believers, we just might see the army of God and the presence of Jesus. In these moments, human limitations are shattered, fear is crushed, and boldness courses through our veins. We begin to take reckless steps of faith, because we know that God is near and he is faithful!

After thirteen years of serving a wonderful church just south of Grand Rapids, Michigan, God called my wife and me to enter a new season of ministry. From a human standpoint, it made no sense. We were in a healthy and growing church. We were serving with a team that we loved, and there was peace in the fabric of the church. People were coming to faith in Jesus and growing in spiritual maturity. We had wonderful friends in the church and the surrounding community. I was part of a network of pastors who prayed for each other and joyfully supported each other's ministry. And the church allowed me to take the time I needed to be away each year so that I could write and continue my speaking ministry. In short, it was a perfect situation!

Then, out of the blue, during a worship service at a church in the Chicago area where I was a guest preacher, God told both my wife and me it was time to move on from this amazing place of ministry. The problem is, he did not tell us where we were going and what would be next. In a matter of months we had processed this clear call of God with the staff, church board, and congregation. We still did not know exactly what God had planned for us.

To an outside observer, this move would have made no sense. To some of my friends in ministry, the decision did not compute. From a financial perspective, it could have been disastrous. To be honest, from a strictly human perspective, I did not understand why I was doing what I was doing.

Sherry and I knew God had spoken to us. We could not see the end game, but we could see God! We did not know what ministry I would serve next, but we were confident Jesus was on the throne and in charge of our future. We kept our eyes on Jesus and were absolutely certain he was leading us. That had to be enough.

If we had looked only at the army that surrounded us and focused on all the challenges we might face in the coming months, we would have never taken this step. Instead, we strained to see the army of God surrounding us and moved forward with assurance that God was leading. With the passing days and weeks, we grew bold and faith-filled. This happened not because we had our future all figured out but because we knew God was going ahead of us and preparing the way. He was leading. This brought a confidence that moved us to take more steps of reckless faith than we would have ever dreamed.

Where are your eyes focused? Are you fixated on the enemy army surrounding the city, the dark economic times, the people who resist the will of God in this world, the greatness of your own sin, your physical limitations, or a laundry list of other fear-producing realities in this crazy world? If you are, you know what it feels like to be spiritually paralyzed!

Dare to pray, "Open my eyes so I can see." As you do, you will discover that the army of the Lord still stands at attention, awaiting the command of heaven. Jesus is still on the throne. God is still powerful beyond our comprehension. You are never alone. God is closer than you think, ready to move in ways we cannot imagine or dream. When we get a glimpse of this, we move from fear and frustration to bold and reckless faith.

Let My Heart Feel What You Feel

It is easy to buffer and protect our hearts. In a world filled with pain, poverty, abuse, addictions, and countless ills and evils, sometimes it feels better when we can look the other way and not face the cold, harsh realities all around us. If ignorance is bliss, we can ensure our happiness by simply looking the other way and acting like everything around us is fine. By doing this we can avoid the pain of seeing people's suffering. If we keep our hearts hard, we don't have to deal with the anguish of knowing there are children dying of hunger, women being sold as sex slaves, Christians being killed for their faith, and entire people groups who have not yet heard the great news of Jesus.

Bob Pierce was a young man who had a passion to spread the good news of Jesus. After being trained in the wonderful evangelistic organization Youth for Christ, he decided to travel to China and share the message and hope of Jesus.[15] Along the way he was exposed to the shocking reality of poverty in the world. In particular, Pierce was captivated by the plight of children who were living and dying with hunger. One day he wrote this prayer inside the cover of his Bible: *Let my heart be broken by the things that break the heart of God.*

The God of heaven answered this prayer over and over again. Pierce lived as a man broken by the pain and suffering of others. This led him to reckless faith that moved him to begin an organization called World Vision[16] around 1950 and later another ministry called Samaritan's Purse[17] around 1970. Though Bob Pierce died and went to be with Jesus in 1978, both of these ministries are thriving today, and millions of children around the world continue to receive care, food, and the message of God's love revealed in Jesus Christ through ministries started by the reckless faith of one man. I am convinced that the prayer Robert Pierce wrote in his Bible became a catalyst for change in his heart, life, and then the world.

What might happen in our lives if we begin to pray, "Let my heart feel what you feel, O God"? What action of faith might be born in and through us if we allow the broken heart of Jesus to fill and guide us? When Jesus came to the city of Bethany to see his friends Mary, Martha, and Lazarus, he knew exactly what he was going to do. Jesus was going to raise Lazarus from the dead. We read that, as he observed the grief and sorrow of people he cared deeply about, "Jesus wept."[18]

This is the shortest verse in the Bible, but one filled with profound truth. Jesus, God in human flesh, felt deeply. God weeps! So should we! If we begin to ask God to let our heart beat with his heart, we will be moved to open our eyes and see the pain, brokenness, and needs all around us. We will feel at a whole new level, as we experience genuine discomfort, pain, and even anguish over the things that people in our world face every day.

This is reckless prayer that moves us to costly and faithful actions. Will you dare to pray and ask God to let your heart feel what he feels? Do you have the courage to invite discomfort and even deep pain as God makes your heart more like his own? This is a reckless prayer that could change you and, in turn, impact the world in powerful ways.

There are many wonderful ways to pray. Countless books have been written to help us dig in and communicate with God in fresh new ways. The question is *not*, will you pray?

Most people do. The real issue is, will you lift up reckless prayers? Imagine what might happen if you made these prayers part of your normal day:

Your will be done.
Grow your fruit.
Speak, Lord, your servant is listening.
Open our eyes so we can see.
Let my heart feel what you feel.

Reflections on Responsible Recklessness

In each chapter of this book we have focused on what I call responsible recklessness. God calls us to reckless faith, but he also wants us to be wise. This is why we use the simple matrix of prayer, perspective, and patience each time we feel led to put reckless faith into action. These three ideas help us walk forward with both boldness and wisdom.

When it comes to reckless prayer, we must lean heavily on the second part of this matrix. We need to gain biblical perspective. As we pray, "Your will be done," we can be confident that God has revealed his will in the pages of Scripture.

As we pray, "Grow your fruit," we are asking for his character and qualities to blossom in our lives. We do not have to make up some new standards or a human checklist of religious attitudes. God has already spelled it out for us: love, joy, peace, patience, kindness, goodness, faithfulness, gentleness, and self-control. There you have it! Build your prayers around the specific fruits God wants to grow in your life and the lives of those you love.

Each time you pray, "Speak, Lord, your servant is listening," you are asking the Good Shepherd to direct you. Listen well. Pay attention. Take action. And always test every whisper, nudge, prompting, and word against the unchanging truth of the Bible. If you hear something that is contrary to the clear teaching of Scripture, it is not from the Lord! The still small voice of the Spirit will always direct you in a way that is consistent with the revealed will of God in the Bible.

As you learn to pray, "Open my eyes so I can see," the teaching of Scripture guides here as well. God will not lead us to see things that are contrary to his character and nature revealed in the pages of the Old and New Testaments. Consistency is the key. God is eternally the same. Any picture or vision you have of him will ring true with the vision God has revealed in his Holy Word.

Finally, as you pray, "Let my heart feel what you feel," this tug and brokenness will look like the heart of God revealed through the whole story of the Bible. As we study the Old Testament, we discover that God has a special place in his heart for the outcast, broken, fatherless, widow, traveler from another land, and all those who are hurting and marginalized.[19] This same theme permeates the New Testament as we see the heart of Jesus break for those who are hurting and outcast.[20] A broken heart is not something we have to invent or create. Our model is the God of the universe who loves tenderly and cares more deeply than we ever could. The key is that our heart would reflect the broken heart of God.

With all of these reckless prayers, we are wise to gain solid biblical perspective and let the clear teaching of the Bible direct and shape both our prayers and our actions. This will lead to responsible recklessness for the glory of God.

Diving into Reckless Prayers

» **Praying Reckless Prayers**

Spend time on your own, or with other Christians, and pray in some of the following directions:

- Your will be done.
- Grow your fruit in my life and the lives of the people I love.
- Speak, Lord, your servant is listening . . . and help me take time to listen.
- Open my eyes so I can see.
- I pray for my friends who are going through a tough time—open their eyes so they can see your presence and power, O Lord.
- Let my heart feel what you feel and move me to action that is consistent with your desire for me.
- Help me read and know your Word so that I can test everything against your eternal and unchanging truth.

» **Taking Reckless Actions**

Pray, "Let my heart feel what you feel." Allow yourself to be swept into the compassion and love of God's heart. When this happens, you will begin to notice broken people, those who are outcast, the forgotten and least in this world (and in your own community). Be open for God to call you to some kind of action, sacrifice, or commitment to give of yourself and your resources.

When this happens, tell a few friends who can pray with you and keep you accountable to act on what is happening in your heart. Let your emotions get engaged, but also take action. Do something that is consistent with how God is moving in your heart.

As you seek to grow in compassion and the love of God, you might even want to write this simple prayer inside the cover of your Bible. It is the prayer offered by Bob Pierce so many years ago: *Let my heart be broken by the things that break the heart of God.*

» Thinking Reckless Thoughts

Reflect on some of these questions in the coming days:

- Do I tend to pray more "My will be done" prayers than "Thy will be done" prayers? How can I focus more on the will of God in my prayer life?
- What fruit of the Spirit needs to grow in my life during this particular season? What fruits need to grow in the lives of those I care about?
- What is a fruit of the Spirit that has been growing in my life and how can I celebrate and rejoice in this good growth?
- When was the last time I heard a whisper from God and how did I respond to God's leading?
- How can I make listening for God a more regular and normative part of my daily routine?
- How might I live with greater boldness and God-honoring recklessness if I had an awareness of God's presence, power, and glory around me each moment?
- How might my attitude and lifestyle change if my heart was beating and breaking with the heart of God?

8

reckless words

Our oldest son, Zach, was only six years old when he walked up to Sherry and said, "Mom, I am going to tell you something and don't say what you always say!"

Over the previous year, Zach had come to both Sherry and me a few times and said, "I want to be a pastor when I grow up." Sherry had consistently responded the same way. She said, "That is great. We would love it if you became a pastor someday, but you have a lot of time to figure out what you want to do with your life." Both Sherry and I have been very careful not to push or pressure our sons to go into full-time Christian service unless God is clearly calling them.

That particular day Zach had been reading a large section of his first-grade-reader children's Bible and felt a strong sense that he would be a pastor someday. He wanted to declare this to his mom without hearing the "We'll wait and see" speech again. He asked her not to say what she always said, then he told her, one more time, "I want to be a pastor someday." From that time on, we never questioned him about it.

It has been nearly two decades since that encounter, and today our son Zach works full-time in the church in the areas of worship and young adult ministry. He is also halfway through his Master of Divinity program and still desires to give his life in service to God.

Our words are powerful! They can be tame and safe, or bold and reckless. Even at six years old we can begin to speak reckless words.

Committed to Reckless Words! Really?

There are all kinds of reckless words. In my book *Seismic Shifts*, I wrote a whole chapter about using our words to build others up and not to tear them down. I wrote another chapter about speaking the truth in love. These are very important topics that could be addressed here, but I want us to turn our attention toward what I believe is the most powerful topic for reckless words: the good news of God revealed in Jesus.

As followers of the Savior, we have received his words of life. We have been cleansed. We have entered an eternal friendship with Jesus. We have come to know the One who is the way, the truth, and the life.[1] We have a message to share with the world. Our words should be seasoned with the salt of God's truth and love.[2]

Many Christians today declare a personal commitment to reaching out with the love of Jesus and sharing the good news of salvation in his name. But too many of them don't act on this conviction. Over the past twenty years, my wife and I have written over seventy small group studies in partnership with some of the best pastors, leaders, scholars, and Christian writers of our generation.[3] These studies cover almost every topic of the faith you can imagine: parenting, marriage, love, serving, the Lord's Prayer, authentic relationships, essentials of the faith, intimacy, the Holy Spirit, joy, and the list goes on. One of these studies focuses on the important topic of sharing our faith.

Every three months we receive a report of how many copies of each of these studies have been sold. Take a wild guess which one is consistently the lowest-selling study, quarter after quarter. Unfortunately, it is the one about evangelism.

Christians of virtually every brand and stripe declare with bold confidence that they are committed to the work of the Great Commission.[4] They say it in a variety of ways, but almost all churches express a serious commitment to outreach, evangelism, sharing faith, mission, and reaching the world with the gospel. At the same time, so many believers are afraid to take action on this commitment. They look at it as something awkward and uncomfortable. That is why I have spent the past twenty years helping Christians and churches learn to do organic outreach.[5] It is all about sharing our faith in ways that feel natural and comfortable—for us and for the people we seek to reach with the grace and truth of the Savior.

In our culture today, one of the boldest and most important things a follower of Jesus can do as they live with reckless faith is to put their convictions into words. Reckless words about Jesus and his good news can make an eternal difference in the lives of those we encounter every day. Sharing our faith and articulating the love, grace, and message of Jesus is one of the most reckless things we could ever do.

Every time we take a bold step of faith and share the truth of Jesus, we enter a war zone. This is a place of spiritual battle. It is the realm of heavenly warfare. It is a laboratory for reckless faith!

The apostle Paul gave this exhortation:

> Finally, be strong in the Lord and in his mighty power. Put on the full armor of God so that you can take your stand against the devil's schemes. For our struggle is not against flesh and blood, but against the rulers, against the authorities, against the powers of this dark world and against the spiritual forces of evil in the heavenly realms. Therefore put on the full armor of God, so that when the day of evil comes, you may be able to stand your ground. (Eph. 6:10–13)

When we make a decision to tell our story of faith, share the message of the gospel of Jesus, or enter into spiritual conversations with people who are not followers of Jesus, the battle is on!

Every Christian should be connecting with people who are not yet followers of Jesus. Just like the Savior, we should have many friendships with those who have not received his grace. Our lives should be an example of kindness and passionate love. We should serve freely and be examples of reckless generosity. But friendship and being an example is *not* enough.

We are also called to speak words of life. We are to be his witnesses, and this means more than just living a good life. No matter how good our life might be, we must articulate the message of faith in Jesus. Words, reckless and beautiful words, need to be expressed. They can be texted, tweeted, or emailed. We can communicate the gospel through a casual chat on the phone, face-to-face at work, between classes at school, or over a cup of coffee. Followers of Jesus who are committed to a reckless life of faith will learn to communicate words that offer the love, grace, and life-saving truth that is found in Jesus Christ alone.

Thankful for Reckless Words

My journey to Jesus was paved with the reckless words of Christians who dared to express truth, love, and the gospel to me. God placed a whole parade of people in my life who dared to articulate the nature of their friendship with Jesus and the content of the message that had transformed their lives.

I am thankful my sister Gretchen came to faith in Jesus and did not keep it to herself. She began to tell me about her relationship with the Savior, she invited me to events at her youth group, and she validated her words with a life that was being transformed by God. I could see it. But I could also hear the truth as she spoke.

God placed a young man named Doug Drainville in my life. He was only a few years older than me, but his commitment to serve and befriend me opened the door for many conversations about how his life had changed since entering a relationship with Jesus. Doug always seemed to have a story about how God was working in his life, helping him through a struggle, or giving him strength to press on. I did not find his stories and declarations of faith bothersome. They were a natural part of who Doug was. God used his reckless words to shape my journey toward Jesus.

I will be eternally grateful for the words spoken by Doug Fields and Gary Webster, two leaders at the houseboat ministry I attended the summer I became a follower of Jesus. I went on the summer trip with the intention of water skiing and hanging out with some new friends. By the end of the week on the Sacramento Delta, they extended an invitation to confess my sins, receive God's grace, and enter a life-saving relationship with Jesus.

Since that week, I have never been the same.

In each of these situations, and far more than I have space to tell about, there was a real person who loved me enough to put their faith into words. They took a chance and got a little reckless. When they dared to speak, God infused their words with the presence and power of his Holy Spirit and moved me forward in my adventure of faith.

If we are going to take a journey of reckless faith, our words will be an important part of the story. We must get past the fears, lies, and deception of the enemy. We need to become like the kid in the small-town parade who throws candy with two-fisted fury. We need to spread the seed of the gospel everywhere we go and with everyone we meet. We need to become like the farmer in Jesus's parable who does not study the soil and try to determine if conditions are perfect. Rather, we need to throw seed freely and generously. We can be confident that the seed bag of God's grace, love, and good news will never be empty. The more we throw, the more there is!

Faith Comes by Hearing

It is never enough to just live a good life and hope people figure out who Jesus is. We are called to articulate the faith and speak reckless words of life. The apostle Paul puts it this way:

How, then, can they call on the one they have not believed in? And how can they believe in the one of whom they have not heard? And how can they hear without someone preaching to them? And how can they preach unless they are sent? As it is written, "How beautiful are the feet of those who bring good news!" (Rom. 10:14–15)

We are to be prepared to express, with clear, gentle, and bold words, the amazing grace and hope we have experienced in Jesus: "But in your hearts set apart Christ as Lord. Always be prepared to give an answer to everyone who asks you to give the reason for the hope that you have. But do this with gentleness and respect."[6] Don't you love those words? "Gentleness and respect." We are not to force it on people or beat them over the head. We are to speak with bold clarity and gentle respect.

Can I Tell You My Story?

We all have a story to tell and one of the best ways to express the great news of God's love and salvation in Jesus is by simply telling it. The truth is, we don't have just one story, but many. Each of us has been transformed by the presence and grace of Jesus. We need to be willing to share how a friendship with the Savior has changed us for the better.

I was preparing a Sunday morning message to preach at Shoreline Community Church, and I wanted to help people feel more comfortable sharing their story of how God had entered their life by the leading of the Holy Spirit and transformed them through the grace of Jesus. As I prayed for God's leading, it came to me. I knew exactly what I needed to share. I knew I had to call some of our leaders and get their permission before I told part of their story from the pulpit.

At the end of the message, I told the congregation, "You need to know something about four of your pastors. One of them served time in San Quentin State Prison (not as a visitor but as an inmate). Another one of your pastors was a methamphetamine addict before he knew Jesus. Another was raised in an athe-istic home with no faith in God. He never heard the name of Jesus except when someone was angry. One of your pastors was homeless and had a time when he lived on the streets, in a car, or on the couches of friends who would take him in."

I did not tell the congregation which of their pastors matched up with each story. I did encourage them to talk with us and figure it out. I closed the service by saying, "God has called, has forgiven, and is using an ex-con, an ex-drug addict, an ex-atheist, and someone who was homeless as the pastors of your church." Then I said, "Shoreline Church, these are your pastors!"

The entire congregation broke into spontaneous applause! I did not plan this or expect it. How could I have? This response was repeated at all three Sunday morning services. There was a sense of excitement and joyful relief when the congregation realized that all their pastors are simply forgiven sinners who are being changed by God's presence.

When we tell our story of God's transforming grace, pres-ence, and power, these reckless words have a life-changing impact!

Our Conversion Story

One way to share our story is by simply telling about how we came to faith in Jesus. This is *our conversion story*. It is the most common kind of testimony or faith story that Christians are encouraged to tell others. It is a story of who I was before I knew Jesus, how I came to faith in the Savior (including the truth of the gospel I came to embrace), and how my life has changed since I received the grace of Jesus. Some of the best evangelism training programs in the world lead Christians through a process of learning to articulate their conversion story.[7]

We each have our own story of coming to faith in Jesus and experiencing the transforming power of the Holy Spirit. I have told my story many times through the years and am thankful every chance I get to tell it again.

I grew up in a home with a computer programmer father and a schoolteacher mom who taught science and math. I would describe my family as loving, healthy, and agnostic. There was not an aggressive attack on the Christian faith. Religion was simply a nonissue. God was not part of our conversations or family life. I had no idea that Christmas or Easter were religious holidays that had a connection to the story of Jesus. This was not on my radar.

In third grade my friend David got leukemia and died very suddenly. I had never heard of this sickness before, and this was the first person I knew who died. I remember asking some spiritual questions after he passed away. No one seemed to have any helpful answers.

Later, when I was in middle school, I began to ask questions about life, death, and God. I remember standing in the bathroom at home with the lights off, filled with fear and confusion. I wept in the dark for quite a while before my dad knocked on the door and gently asked me what was wrong. We sat down on the edge of my dad's bed and he listened to me talk for about thirty minutes. After I poured out my spiritual questions, my dad told me there are many and various ways people have tried to answer such inquiries through history. He walked over to the bookshelves that lined his bedroom wall and took down a seven-volume set of books on world religions. He handed it to me and informed me that he did not have personal answers to these kinds of questions, but I was welcome to read the thoughts of others.

I took the set of books to my room and flipped through a few pages. The print was very small, the content was dense, the vocabulary was way over the head of a middle school student, and there were no pictures. My foray into the world of religion concluded abruptly as I put the set of books back on my dad's shelf. If my father did not have answers to these questions, I was pretty sure no one did.

For the next four years I jumped into the normal behaviors and attitudes of a California coastal kid. None of this moved me toward Jesus.

When I was in high school, my sister Gretchen began going to Garden Grove Community Church with some of her friends. With time, she became a Christian. She was excited about her faith. Gretchen shared her stories with me and others and even invited me to come to her church youth group. I had absolutely no interest. As a matter of fact, I was quite hostile toward her and responded to her invitations with profanity and a mean spirit. She just continued being nice to me, telling me about what a difference her newfound faith was making in her life, and she extended offers to give me a ride to her youth group activities. She told me the people there were very cool and friendly. I wanted nothing to do with it.

Finally, Gretchen came with one more invitation. She gave a preamble before inviting me and said, "Don't say no until you hear what is happening at my youth group." She went on to explain that her church youth group was going to be having a Casino Night with blackjack tables, roulette wheels, poker, and a twenty-girl cancan dance line.[8]

For the first time in my life, church sounded like fun!

I told my sister I would come to her youth event. I showed up with two of my friends who were as far away from Jesus as I was.

It was all true! The gambling, the girls, and about a thousand high school students showed up for the big Casino Night. I had a blast. I even sat and listened when the youth pastor gave a quick little message. It was something like "Life's a Gamble, Where Are You Putting Your Chips?" While I was at the youth event, I met a cute blonde girl and decided I should go back the next week.

I kept attending the youth group, mostly to see the cute blonde girl. I did pay attention and listen to some of what the youth pastor talked about. I found it interesting but was not ready to sign on the dotted line.

When summer came, I signed up to go on a weeklong water-skiing trip. The cute blonde girl and I were the only people on the trip who were not yet followers of Jesus. Let's just say the odds were stacked against us. To top it off, we were floating on a houseboat in the Sacramento Delta. There was no getting away.

Every day the leaders on the boat would lead morning Bible studies, sing a bunch of Christian songs with the students, and then have a message in the evening. I did not really feel trapped or pressured. I just kept listening and watching these young people who seemed absolutely serious about their faith. They talked about Jesus like he was a personal friend. They had been changed through their relationship with him. It was clear to see.

On the last evening of the houseboat water-skiing trip, one of the leaders shared the simple story of Jesus. He explained that God loves us all more than we could possibly know or understand. But we have each turned away from him by our decision to sin and do things, think things, and say things that are against God's perfect plan for us. That part made sense to me. I was very aware that I was doing things that were very wrong. He went on to tell about how God came into human history on Christmas, when Jesus was born. Jesus lived a life with no sin or wrong and he died in our place and for our sins on the cross. He knew all the wrongs we had ever done and would ever do and still loved us. Jesus paid the price to cleanse us from sin and restore us to a healthy friendship with God. He explained that Jesus not only died on the cross, but three days after he was buried, Jesus rose again—that was what Easter was all about.

I listened to the whole story and appreciated this guy's passion and certainty about all this God stuff. The fact is, I had a lot more questions than I had answers, and I was not even sure if most of what the boat leader said was true. The part that made the most sense to me was the reality of my own wrongs and sins.

The boat captain asked if anyone wanted to receive Jesus that night. It was a bit comical, because the only two people on the boat who were not Christians were me and the cute blonde girl. Everyone knew this. He extended the offer and asked if anyone was ready to pray and confess their sins, asking Jesus to cleanse them so they could begin a whole new life following Jesus.

I can still remember my prayer. I did not grow up around any of this religious activity, so it was all new to me. I prayed something like, "God, I am not totally sure you are out there. I don't know if what I have heard about Jesus is even true. But if you really love me like these people say, and if you really died on the cross for me, and if you can wash me clean and give me a new life, you can have me and I will put my faith in you." I confessed lots of wrong attitudes, words, and actions. Then I prayed for God to forgive me and invited Jesus to take over my life. I did my best to surrender to him.

It is hard to explain what happened next. Everything changed. That very night God called me to spend my life telling others about his love, and I made a commitment to be a pastor. This was quite a shock to my parents, who were certainly not anticipating that their eldest son would become a man of the cloth. God really did enter my heart, wash me clean, and set my life on a new trajectory.

When I think of the day I made a decision to follow Jesus, I realize that I did not have a lot of the answers. The fact is, I still have plenty of questions and I'm a pastor! I was not one of those people who studied for years and solved all of the intellectual objections to Christianity (though I believe the Christian faith does hold up under rigorous intellectual scrutiny). I knew enough to put my trust in Jesus, and he has been leading me ever since.

When people look at me and ask, how did a guy who grew up in a home like yours become a pastor? I tell them, "Here is the short version: I went for the gambling, I stayed for the women, and I found Jesus!" That's my story and I'm sticking to it!

My story is just that—my story. It is unique to me.

My wife gave her heart to Jesus when she was five years old. She can remember what her mom was cooking on the kitchen stove that Sunday afternoon she asked Jesus to be her Savior. She could describe where she was lying on the living room couch as she invited Jesus into her heart. My brother Jason resisted for many years but finally, through a lot of reading, many discussions, and rigorous academic grappling, placed his trust in Jesus and followed the Savior. There is not a right or wrong story—you have yours and I have mine. We should tell it often and let people know when and how we became a follower of Jesus.

In the book of Acts, we hear the story of the apostle Paul's conversion over and over again.[9] Paul loved to tell others about how he came to follow the Savior and the difference Jesus made in his life. There is something powerful about asking someone, "Can I tell you my story?" If they say yes, you can share who you were before knowing Jesus, how you came to faith in him, and what has happened in your life since that transforming moment.

Our Stories of God's Power

Not only do we need to freely tell the story of when we first came to faith in Jesus, but it is critical that we recklessly tell stories about how God is working in our life right now. These *testimonies of the power of God* speak volumes to people who wonder if this whole faith thing is for real. Here is a simple truth I have learned after more than three decades of interacting with close family and friends who are not yet in a relationship with Jesus: many people outside of the faith do not believe that we believe what we say we believe.

Let me state that again, and read these words slowly. Many non-Christians looking at you and me do not believe that we believe what we say we believe.

Some people who have not embraced the grace of Jesus look at Christians and think we are playing some kind of religious game. They imagine that we go to church and get just enough religion to appease some sense of personal guilt. They suspect that we are not really serious about this whole "relationship with God" thing. People look at us from a distance and don't have any idea how real, deep, and personal our faith is.

When we tell a current life story about how God has shown up and revealed his love and power in a tangible way, this speaks to people. It shows them God is real, alive, and able to make a difference in our daily life. The beauty of this kind of personal story of faith is that we don't just have one testimony. These stories are being written every day. As God shows up and reveals his power and mighty hand to provide for, protect, and lead us, we have more stories to share.

We might have one story about when and how we became a follower of Jesus, but we have many stories about God's power in our lives. Be generous and reckless in telling these stories about God's amazing work in your life ten years ago, ten weeks ago, and ten hours ago. These testimonies can be about big and amazing things or simple ways God works. They just need to be authentic and capture the real and un-deniable hand of God in your life.

When Sherry and I were first married, we struggled finan-cially. By our second year of marriage, we were both in sem-inary full-time, I was working in a local ministry full-time, and Sherry was volunteering significant time at that same church. I had grown up being taught that when things are tough, you just work harder and everything will take care of itself. The problem was, we were already working as hard as we could and were still not keeping our heads above water. As our financial situation grew more desperate, we prayed harder. We cried out, "God, please provide what we need. Help!" We were not asking for extras but enough to stop going deeper into debt.

A short time later, there was a knock on the door of our little apartment in Pasadena. It was Marc, a dear Christian friend I had not seen in almost a year. I was so glad to see him and invited him in. When I asked what brought him up to Pasadena, he said, in a matter-of-fact way, "The other day I was spending some time reading the Bible and praying. God put you on my heart and let me know that I should give you some money every month until you are out of school."

We had been praying so we should not have been so surprised, but we were. Sherry and I wept as Marc shared his story and handed us an envelope. I can't even remember the exact amount of money he gave, but that was not the point. We felt the power and provision of God and knew he was taking care of us. This has become one of our testimonies.

Another time God showed his power by giving very specific direction. When we moved to Monterey, we entered a whole new world of housing costs. As I shared earlier in the book, I thought Sherry and I would always live in apartments or church-owned homes. I never really planned on getting a house. When we moved from Michigan, our house was paid off, but the full value of the house was equal to a down payment on a house in Monterey. We had no idea what we were going to do. As we began looking at house options, we were staggered by the prices and had a hard time finding a place we could afford that also had the space we needed. Two or three times we tried to move forward on what we thought was a great option and the doors kept slamming in our face. In one situation, we made three offers on the same house and were rejected every time. It would have been comedic if it were not so painful.

Finally, God opened the door for the perfect house for us. It was about three hundred yards from the house we had made multiple offers on and experienced three rejections. We would have never imagined we could get this house, but in twenty-four hours, the deal fell together. Only God could have made this work. After months of battling to find a place, God gently set one in our lap in less than a day. What a testimony to his powerful guidance!

Sometimes the stories of God's power are not the shocking and grandiose occurrences, but the little ways God enters in and takes care of us. It can be a check that comes in the mail right when you need it, wise counsel from a godly friend that gives you confidence in a tough situation, a call that you got the job just when you thought you were off the short list, or even a sermon preached at church that you just know was meant for you. All of these are rich soil for giving a testimony of God's power and provision.

Our Stories of God's Presence

In a similar way, we can tell *personal stories of God's presence* in the good and hard times of life. Nonbelievers wonder if our faith makes a difference. When we tell them about a time God drew near to us and brought his comfort and care, this reveals the reality that we know God. We are not playing an empty religious game, but God is completely real to us. He is closer than our best friends.

When my wife was in college, she moved from the small town of Holland, Michigan, to a big state university campus. She describes this season as one of the loneliest times in her life. She left a town where it seemed everyone knew each other and moved to a place where she was a stranger with no common history. To top it off, her roommates in her dorm lived a very different lifestyle and Sherry felt excluded and ostracized. If you ask her about that season of her life, Sherry would be honest about the difficulty and loneliness she experienced, but she would tell you that God became her lifeline and closest friend in this very challenging season. This is an example of a testimony of God's presence.

When we moved from Michigan to California, both Sherry and I said good-bye to friendships that had been built over twenty years. Sherry was leaving family and friends she had known from her childhood. God drew near and showed his presence and care in this challenging time of transition. His comfort and care was more real and substantial than anything another person could offer. This has become a testimony of God's presence that we share with others who are in the midst of a life transition.

Give it a try sometime. Ask a person the simple question, "Can I tell you about how I became a follower of Jesus?" If they are open to listen, share about that life-changing time you first understood the truth of God's love and grace and accepted Jesus to be your Savior. Let them know how this decision and new friendship has transformed your life. Look for opportunities to share stories of how God has shown up in power in your life, providing, delivering, protecting, and guiding you. And rejoice as you share stories of how you have experienced God's loving presence in the great moments and the hard times. Telling these stories can be some of the most reckless words you ever speak.

Can I Tell You His Story?

Telling our stories should be a normal part of our conversational life. People with reckless faith love to find natural and organic occasions to talk about God's presence, power, and the salvation that comes through Jesus Christ. As we learn to share our testimony and people see that our faith is deep, personal, and authentic, we can go a bit deeper. We dare to ask the next logical question, "Can I tell you the story of Jesus?"

Our story is a tangible unfolding of who God is and what he has done in our life. But people need to meet Jesus for themselves. There comes a time when we take the risk to be reckless and ask if we can share the life-changing message of Jesus.

In my book *Organic Outreach for Ordinary People*, I walk through six distinct ways to tell the story of Jesus.[10] There are many great books and resources to help you share the simple and powerful message of the gospel.[11] There is no right way or wrong way. But there is a simple message that each of us can communicate. The apostle Paul, inspired by the Holy Spirit, put it this way:

Now, brothers, I want to remind you of the gospel I preached to you, which you received and on which you have taken your stand. By this gospel you are saved, if you hold firmly to the word I preached to you. Otherwise, you have believed in vain.

For what I received I passed on to you as of first importance: that Christ died for our sins according to the Scriptures, that he was buried, that he was raised on the third day according to the Scriptures. (1 Cor. 15:1–4)

You can share the whole message of the good news of Jesus in less than a minute. It is not that complicated. Of course we can add Bible passages and illustrations, but the basic message it quite simple. Read this little section below and time how long it takes to share this message.

The good news and story of Jesus is pretty simple.

God loves us more than we dream or imagine, and he wants to be in a close and growing friendship with us.

All human beings have acted in ways that break our relationship with God and make it impossible for us to find our way back to him. The Bible calls this sin. Sin is anything we think, say, or do that is not in line with God's good and perfect will. We also sin in those moments when we know we should do something good but fail to act on it. The truth is, we have all sinned a lot.

God loves people so much that he went on a mission to bring us back into a healed and healthy relationship with him. God came among us as a little human baby boy, Jesus. This is what Christmas is all about.

Jesus lived a life with no sin, wrong, or evil. He was perfect in every way. But he went to the cross and paid the price of a common criminal so that he could take our sin and punishment upon himself. Jesus did not have to die on the cross. It was his choice, a gift of love.

After Jesus died on the cross, he was buried and then he rose from the grave three days later. This is what we celebrate at Easter. In his resurrection, Jesus broke the power of sin, death, and the grave. His sacrifice and resurrection opened the way for us to have a restored relationship with God.

Our part is to believe and receive. We believe this simple story and message of God's love and grace. Then, we confess our sins and receive the forgiveness that can only come through the sacrificial gift of Jesus. When this happens, Jesus becomes both our Savior and the Leader of our life. He cleanses us and restores our relationship to the Father. He leads us for the rest of our life and for eternity.

Of course, there is far more that can be shared. There are lots of great Bible passages you can read and discuss with a friend who is open to hear the story of Jesus.[12] This simple presentation of the message of Jesus covers the core truths and it takes about a minute and a half to communicate. I don't encourage people to memorize this presentation of the gospel but to make sure they have the key elements in their heart as they put it in their own words. Here are the essentials when telling the story of Jesus:

1. God is loving.
2. We have all sinned and are separated from God.
3. The solution to our sin problem is Jesus, and Jesus alone.
4. Jesus was God among us and he really lived, died for our sins, and rose again from the grave in glory.
5. We can believe and receive God's gift of grace through faith in Jesus!

Do You Want to Know More about Jesus?

If we are prayerful and love the people in our lives who are not followers of Jesus, we will find ourselves telling our stories and his story in the flow of our natural conversations. All of us are bound to encounter people who are not ready to receive Jesus as their Savior and Leader, but they may be open to having spiritual conversations. What do we do in these moments?

I would suggest you ask this reckless question: "Do you want to know more about Jesus?" Most will say, "Yes." Some might say, "No thank you." In either case, you get a sense of where they are on their spiritual journey.

This question is reckless because you are inviting a spiritual seeker to dig in and go deeper in their understanding of who Jesus is and what he did. It is also reckless because you are committing yourself to walk with them on this journey. You might begin a weekly Bible study with this friend or family member.[13] It could mean getting a good book on apologetics for an intellectual or skeptical friend and discussing it with them.[14] You might invite them to be part of a small group that makes spiritual seekers comfortable and provides a place for them to learn and ask questions about faith. This might be a perfect time to invite them to your church if this is a place where they will be loved, accepted, and embraced in a grace-filled community. There are many ways to continue the spiritual conversation.

Every time we ask someone the reckless question, "Do you want to know more about Jesus?" we make a commitment to walk with them and invest in their journey toward the Savior. There are few things more exciting and meaningful.

Would You Like to Receive Jesus as Your Leader and Savior?

There comes a moment, in many relationships, when it is time to ask a person if they are ready to confess their sins and receive the grace that only Jesus can offer. This often comes after weeks, months, or sometimes years of prayer, conversations, and relationship. There is a time when you look at a spiritually curious person and know in your heart that this just might be the moment their whole eternity could change.

At times like this, the forces of hell rise up and try to keep a person from crying out to Jesus. This is a God-ordained moment, and we need to have the courage to look in the eyes of our friend or family member and ask, "Would you like to receive Jesus? Are you ready? Can I pray with you?"

The story is told of a husband and wife who were talking about sharing their faith with nonbelieving friends. The husband told his wife, "When it comes to that time when I know I should invite a person to pray and receive Jesus as Savior, my hands get all sweaty and my mouth gets as dry as cotton." His wife looked at him with a playful smile and said, "When that happens, just lick your palms and start talking!"

As you grow reckless with your words, you will have spiritual conversations with people who are open to Jesus. You will get reckless and tell your stories of faith. As the Holy Spirit leads, you will share the simple and powerful story of the gospel. You will look into the face of your friend, a family member, or a person you are just getting to know and you will sense they are ready to embrace God's grace offered in Jesus. When this moment comes, don't let a dry mouth or personal anxiety get in the way. Just look into their eyes and ask, "Would you like to receive Jesus as the One who will forgive all your wrongs and lead your life?"

If they indicate they are ready, invite them to pray. Ask if you can lead them through a simple prayer to God.

There are two basic ways to lead in this prayer. First, if you have been walking with them over an extended period of time and they have a good understanding of their sin, their need, and the message of Jesus, you can simply give them prompts and let them form their own prayer. Here is an example of leading someone through this kind of prayer:

Praying with Simple Prompts

1. Take a moment and thank Jesus for what you have been learning about him.

2. Talk to him about your sins. Confess that you have done wrong in your words, actions, and thoughts and admit that you need his forgiveness.

3. Thank God for coming to this world as one of us on that first Christmas. Tell Jesus you are aware that he really came to earth, he lived a perfect life without sin, he died on the cross for your sins, and he rose again from the dead.

4. Ask Jesus to enter your life, cleanse all your wrongs, and lead you from this point on . . . for the rest of your life.

You can give other simple prompts as the Holy Spirit leads you. After they have asked Jesus to cleanse them and enter their life, you can pray. Thank God for their commitment to Jesus, rejoice in their new life of faith, and pray for them to have power to walk with Jesus each day.

In some cases you might feel that the person you are sharing with needs more direction as they pray. You can ask, "Would it be all right for me to lead you through a simple prayer to receive Jesus?" If they say yes, you can ask them to repeat this prayer after you.

Leading in a Simple Prayer

Dear God, I love you
Jesus, I thank you
Holy Spirit, please guide me
I confess my need for Jesus
I have sinned in many ways
I can't cleanse myself
I can't make things right
I cry out to Jesus for forgiveness
Thank you for coming to this world
Thank you for loving me

Thank you for dying on the cross
Thank you for paying the price
Thank you for rising from the dead
Thank you for being here right now
Take charge of my life
Lead me from this moment onward
Teach me to follow you
All the days of my life
And forever
Amen.

Notice that the lines in the prayer are very short. Say each one slowly. Give time for them to do the same. Don't rush this moment. Don't use long, extended lines that are hard to remember. Just walk them through a simple prayer so they can express their desire to enter a real and authentic relationship with God through faith in Jesus, as the Holy Spirit leads.

Feel free to copy this prayer and put it in the back of your Bible, keep a copy in your purse, tuck it into your wallet, or type it as a note in your smartphone. Don't feel like you have to memorize it. Just have it handy when you need it.

Once you have prayed with a person and they have received Jesus, their story is just beginning. Now you can walk with them as they grow in faith. They need to learn how to study the Bible, talk with God in prayer, engage in a Christian church, share their new faith, and grow in many other ways. In the church I serve, we give new believers a copy of a book that walks them through the basics of the Christian faith.[15] We encourage the person who shared the gospel with them or brought them to church to mentor them and help them grow. We also offer a class that walks them through the first steps of walking with Jesus.

What do you do if someone says no when you ask them, "Would you like to receive Jesus as your Leader and Savior?" If they are not ready, don't worry. Just keep the door open and the conversation moving forward. Let them know that as soon as they are ready, they can pray to receive Jesus. They can do this anytime and anywhere. Also let them know that you want to keep talking with them and helping them along. This is not an off-ramp or end to the conversation. It is simply part of walking with people as they move toward the Savior. If they say no, it simply means not yet. Keep praying, sharing your stories of faith, telling the story of Jesus, and loving them. The journey continues.

Reflections on Responsible Recklessness

Many years ago, we were having an open time for students to tell about how they were seeking to be reckless in sharing their faith with others. We had been encouraging people to take chances and speak reckless words of life.

One young person stood up and said, "A group of us got together and tried to be a witness for Jesus." He went on to say, "We ended up getting persecuted for our faith. Someone tried to hit us with a tire iron!" The room fell completely silent. The person leading the discussion asked the pressing question, "How did this happen?"

The students went on to explain their "witnessing tactic." They had gone out in a car with the goal of telling others about Jesus. They would decide, as a group, what slogan or statement they would yell at a passing car or pedestrian. Then they would slow down, lean out the windows, and scream their planned "testimony" at an unsuspecting person and race off.

Apparently they startled and irritated one driver. He grabbed a tire iron from the backseat and raced after them, swinging his arm out his window and trying to hit the hood of their car.

This became an important teachable moment. These students were enthusiastic but irresponsible. They were engaging in sniper behavior, not biblical evangelism. They were not being "persecuted for their faith," but someone was retaliating for their poor behavior. Their example shows that we can be passionate, but do things entirely wrong.

Look again at the wise words of the apostle Peter: "But in your hearts set apart Christ as Lord. Always be prepared to give an answer to everyone who asks you to give the reason for the hope that you have. But do this with gentleness and respect."[16] Do you notice those two important words at the end of the verse? Gentleness. Respect. These are keys to responsible recklessness.

As you prepare to share your story or the story of Jesus with someone, be gentle and respectful. Use the three elements of the matrix discussed in every chapter of this book. First, *pray*. Ask God for the right words and a gentle spirit. (I am confident he will not lead you to scream religious slogans out a moving car window.) Next, gain *perspective*. Read the Bible and watch how Jesus engaged people. He met them where they were and communicated in a way that connected with each person he encountered. You should also get perspective and wise counsel from Christians you respect. If the group of students in this story would have bounced their idea off any of the youth leaders or volunteers, they could have avoided getting dents on the hood of their car. Wise counsel would have prevailed and their enthusiasm could have been directed toward healthy sharing of their faith. Finally, had they just been *patient* and slowed down, had they simply looked at the people they were yelling at and not raced off in their car, they would have seen in their faces that this was not an effective tactic for sharing the message of Jesus.

There are many gentle and winsome ways to share our faith. If we are prayerful, gain wise perspective, and exhibit patience, we will reach out in ways that are bold, reckless, but also respectful. As we do, God will work through us to usher people into the arms of Jesus and the life of his kingdom.

Diving into Reckless Words

>> **Praying Reckless Prayers**

Spend time on your own, or with other Christians, and pray in some of the following directions:

- Thank God for the people he placed in your life who have spoken reckless words of faith and grace to you.
- Pray for courage to share stories of how God has revealed his power in your life. Also ask God to help you tell others about how he is present with you in the good times and in your deepest moments of pain and loss.
- If you have moments when you know God wants you to speak reckless words but your hands get sweaty and your mouth gets as dry as cotton, pray for courage to "lick your palms" and keep talking about Jesus. Ask God to help you press past spiritual opposition and personal fears so that you can speak reckless words about Jesus.
- Pray for the people in your life whom you love, but who do not yet have a friendship with Jesus. Ask for their hearts to be soft to the leading of the Holy Spirit.
- Ask God to bring a revival in the local congregation where you attend, in your denomination (if you are part of one), and in the church all over the world.

>> **Taking Reckless Actions**

Make a copy of the prayer in this chapter (on pages 167–68). Put it in your Bible, in your smartphone, in your wallet, or in your purse. Having this prayer handy and knowing you don't have to memorize it will give you confidence to lead someone in prayer when the moment is right. Ask God to open doors for you to share your story of faith and his story of grace on a regular basis. Pray that you will be bold, when the time is right, to ask a person if they want to pray and receive Jesus as their Savior and the Leader of their life. If they are open, lead them in a prayer and take the next steps to help them grow in faith.

》 Thinking Reckless Thoughts

Reflect on some of these questions in the coming days:

- How did I come to faith in Jesus, and how has my life changed since embracing his grace and friendship? How might I share this story with others?
- How have I experienced the power of Jesus in my life? If I shared stories of God's work in my life from the past and from recent encounters, how might these testimonies inspire others to embrace Jesus?
- What are some ways God has been near me and revealed his presence in my life? How might my testimony of God drawing near me in the tough times of life encourage others to reach out to him in their times of need?
- What are my dry-mouth-and-sweaty-palm moments, and how can I keep sharing Jesus even when I get nervous?
- Who is a nonbeliever I care about whom I need to connect with in the coming days? How could I pray and prepare for this time of potential ministry?

conclusion

The Fruit of a Reckless Life

God left the glory of heaven to come among us. He was born humbly in a stable. Jesus lived a sinless life and he loved with unparalleled compassion. He was crucified and died for you and me. The sinless Son of God was suspended on a Roman cross, beaten, mocked, rejected, and abandoned. He bore our sins and suffered the judgment we deserved. Then he breathed his last breath and died.

The pinnacle of recklessness is seen in the person, life, and death of Jesus Christ. If the story ended when the stone was rolled across the tomb, it would have looked like the most irresponsible act of recklessness in the history of the world.

But three days later, Jesus rose from the grave. The stone was rolled away. He was alive. He *is* alive!

What appeared tragic is now seen as a heavenly act of responsible recklessness that continues to bear fruit for eternity. Heaven has been opened. Death is defeated. Satan is crushed, we are free, and hope is here. Jesus is alive, and we can be too . . . through faith in his name.

Now it is your turn. God invites you to count the cost and take a risk. You can follow in the footsteps of Jesus and live recklessly for the glory of God or you can play it safe.

Can you see the risen Lord inviting you to take a leap?
Are you ready to jump?

The choice is yours, each and every day. If you choose to live a reckless life of faith, you will join Christians all over the world and through the history of the church who have discovered that there is no greater adventure than following the greatest risk taker of all time . . . Jesus.

small group discussion guide

Jesus gathered with small groups of believers and spiritual seekers around tables, in homes, in the open country, and in public settings. He knew there was a powerful dynamic that occurred when people came together to think, talk, study, and pray. As you meet with your small group, be sure to use the teaching DVD content. It will help set the tone and direction for your group and discussion. Use these questions that have been crafted to help you dig into the truth of the Bible, share your life experience together, and create a place for life-impacting application and accountability. My prayer is that the Holy Spirit will show up each time your group gathers and lead you to reckless lives of faith that will honor Jesus and change your world!

In joy,
Kevin G. Harney

Session 1

From Domesticated to Adventurous

Watch: "Introduction" on the *Reckless Faith* DVD

1. Describe some of the ways you have seen our world become more safety conscious and a bit less wild and adventurous through your lifetime.

2. Tell about a time you did something adventurous and exciting in your childhood or adult years. How did you feel as you took this risk and lived on the edge?

3. We all have moments when we dare to follow Jesus and count the cost. Maybe you went on a missions or ministry trip, you gave resources even when it was hard, you shared your faith when you were nervous, you stood up for Jesus when the pressure was on, or you took some other bold step of faith. Tell about a time you took a leap of faith as you followed Jesus and describe how God used this experience to strengthen your relationship with the Savior.

Watch: "Session 1—From Domesticated to Adventurous" on the *Reckless Faith* DVD.

4. What are examples of why some Christians play it safe, resist taking risks, and miss the adventure of faith God has planned for them?

Read: Luke 9:18–25

5. Imagine you were gathered with the disciples of Jesus for this time of prayer and spontaneous teaching. What would the words of Jesus have meant to his disciples in the first century?

6. What might it look like for a Christian in our world today to be willing to do these things Jesus says will be part of following him:
Deny yourself

Take up your cross daily
Follow Jesus
Be willing to lose your life for Jesus

Read: The section titled "Responsible Recklessness Matrix" from this chapter.

7. How can each of the three elements of the reckless faith matrix help a person discern and gain direction for taking steps of reckless faith (or not taking steps of irresponsible recklessness)?
    Praying deeply . . . asking for God's leading and listening for his direction
    Gaining *perspective* (from the Bible and from wise believers)
    Exercising *patience* . . . taking time to reflect, research, and plan

8. What is one bold step of faith or reckless activity you think God has been prompting you to take, but you have still not made the leap? What is standing in the way?

9. How might you use the simple matrix for determining responsible recklessness (the three *P*s) as you consider taking a fresh new step of faith?

10. How can your small group members pray for you, encourage you, and keep you accountable as you consider taking this step of faith?

For prayer direction and additional resources for your group, you might want to review the final section of chapter 1 titled "Diving into Recklessness" on page 22.

Session 2

An Invitation to Reckless Faith

Watch: "Session 2—An Invitation to Reckless Faith" on the *Reckless Faith* DVD

1. Tell about a time you saw a child or adult show reckless generosity and exuberant enthusiasm. How did you feel as you saw this drama unfold?

2. We are children of God through faith in Jesus. How do you think God feels when he sees his children freely share and scatter his love and good news? How do you think he feels when we are overcautious, tentative, and reluctant to share the good news of a life-changing relationship with Jesus?

3. What are some of the reasons we hold back and don't scatter the seeds of God's love, grace, and message as freely as we might want to?

Read: Luke 8:4–15

4. What do you learn about the soil (the hearts and lives of people) as you read this parable?

5. What do you learn about the sower as you read this story? What do you find noteworthy or interesting about this farmer?

Read: 1 Corinthians 3:5–9

6. What is our part in the call to reach the world, and what is God's part? What are some ways we can get this confused and heap too much responsibility on ourselves, and why is this dangerous?

Read: The section titled "We Are Not Smart Enough to Know" from chapter 2

7. Why is it important for us to live with a clear awareness that we can't decide when someone is open and ready to receive Jesus? Can you tell about an example of a person you know who would not have seemed like "good soil" to a casual observer, but God still brought them to himself?

8. Who is a person God has placed in your life who seems hard-hearted and resistant to spiritual things and the message of Jesus? How can you be actively scattering seed in this person's life in the coming weeks? How can your small group members pray for you and encourage you in this relationship?

Read: The section titled "Jesus, Trailblazer of Recklessness!" from this chapter

9. What are some of the ways Jesus has been reckless in his love, kindness, generosity, and grace toward you? How does his example inspire you to be reckless toward others who need to enter a life-giving friendship with the Savior?

For prayer direction and additional resources for your group, you might want to review the final section of chapter 2 titled "Diving into Reckless Faith" on page 35.

Session 3

Reckless Love

Watch: "Session 3—Reckless Love" on the *Reckless Faith* DVD

1. Tell about a person in your life who has sacrificed a great deal for you. How do you feel about this person?

2. What are some of the ways Jesus suffered and sacrificed to show his love to sinful and broken people like you and me? When you reflect on the many ways Jesus has sacrificed for you, how does this grow your love for him?

Read: Romans 5:6–11

3. What do you learn about God's love in this passage?

4. What do you learn about our need for God's love and grace?

Read: 1 John 4:7–12

5. According to John, what is the connection between God's love for us and our love for each other?

6. When you are walking closely with Jesus, how does this impact the way you love and care for family members, friends, and spiritual seekers? When you are not in close fellowship with Jesus and feel far from him, how does this impact your relationships? (Be specific and honest.)

Read: The introduction section from chapter 3 about the gift box

7. Tell about a time in your life when you felt closely connected (bound) to Jesus and you really sensed his love for you. What helped you get to this place of intimacy?

8. How can your group members pray for you and encourage you as you seek to grow an intimate and loving relationship with God? What is one specific step you

need to take to make your walk with Jesus a bigger priority in your life?

Read: Luke 9:23–25

9. What are some specific examples of what it might look like to deny self, take up the cross, and follow Jesus in our daily life?

Read: The section titled "A Picture of Reckless Love" from this chapter

10. What can get in the way of a Christian being willing to suffer for Jesus? What will help us be willing to count the cost and face pain or suffering for the sake of Jesus?

11. What is a situation you are facing that might lead to some kind of suffering if you keep following Jesus? How can your group members pray for you and cheer you on as you seek to lovingly follow Jesus, no matter what the cost?

For prayer direction and additional resources for your group, you might want to review the final section of chapter 3 titled "Diving into Reckless Love" on page 58.

Session 4

Reckless Generosity

Watch: "Session 4—Reckless Generosity" on the *Reckless Faith* DVD

1. Tell about a person you know who has really lived a life of reckless generosity. How has this person's example

impacted you and others who have watched this person's consistent and joyful generosity?

Read: Matthew 6:19–24

2. Right in the middle of the Sermon on the Mount, maybe the most famous sermon in all of human history, Jesus addresses the topic of material things. What warnings do you hear Jesus giving to his followers?

3. What are some of the things we "store up" that can get moth-eaten, become corroded, or be stolen? How much of our life gets invested in gathering, protecting, and taking care of these kinds of things?

4. What can we invest in that truly lasts forever? Be very specific about what you could do in the coming week that will make an eternal impact.

Read: James 1:16–18

5. If every good and perfect gift that we have is truly a gift from our heavenly Father, how should this impact the way we view "our stuff"? How should the spiritual reality that everything is a gift impact how we use the things that are placed in our care?

Read: 1 Timothy 6:17–19

6. What does the apostle Paul teach us about both our attitudes and actions when it comes to the things we have?

7. Give an example of what it might look like, in your life this week, to do *one* of these things (be very specific as to how you might live this out):
For you to be rich in good deeds

For you to be generous
For you to be more willing to share

Read: 1 Timothy 6:6–10

Read: The section titled "Learning Contentment" from this chapter

8. What are signs and behaviors that might indicate a person is *not* living with contentment? What are indicators that we are growing more content?

9. What is one step you could take toward a more content lifestyle, and how might this decision bring greater peace and joy to your life?

10. Jesus was clear that what lasts forever and matters the most in the entire universe is God and people. When we invest in the things of God and the lives of people, we store up treasure in heaven (see Matt. 6:19). What is one eternal investment you are pouring into during this time of your life?

11. What is one way you can increase your eternal investments and pour more into the things of God or the life of a person? How can your group members pray for you and encourage you in your efforts to invest in this heavenly treasure?

For prayer direction and additional resources for your group, you might want to review the final section of chapter 4 titled "Diving into Reckless Generosity" on page 84.

Session 5

Reckless Service

Watch: "Session 5—Reckless Service" on the *Reckless Faith* DVD

1. Tell about a time you saw a Christian offer reckless service. What impact did this humble action make?

2. Share about a time you offered an act of reckless service because you knew God wanted you to do it. How did this experience shape your life? How did it minister to another person?

Read: John 13:1–17

3. What do you learn about the heart and lifestyle of Jesus in this account?

4. What do you learn about Jesus's disciples as you watch their behavior and listen to their words?

5. As followers of Jesus, we receive very specific instructions and exhortation in this passage. What is Jesus saying to all Christians in John 13:12–17? What do you hear him saying to you personally?

6. What gets in the way of your offering humble and consistent acts of service in one of the following circles of your personal influence?
   In your home
   In your neighborhood
   In your workplace or school
   In your community
   In the world

What can you do to break past this barrier to service?

7. Give an example of a practical way you could begin serving in one of these areas:
   In your home
   In your neighborhood
   In your workplace or school
   In your community
   In the world

   How could your group members pray for you, partner with you, and encourage you as you seek to serve in this way?

Read: The section titled "Little Steps of Recklessness" from chapter 5

8. What is one small, but consistent, action of service you could take that would give you a regular reminder of the importance of serving others?

Read: The section titled "Reflections on Responsible Recklessness" from this chapter

9. It is possible to take on too much, overserve, and allow people or needs to control us. When this happens we can become burned out and bitter. Tell about a time this happened to you and how prayer, perspective, and patience could have helped you avoid this pitfall.

10. What have you learned about striking a balance of serving with consistent, reckless passion, but also keeping boundaries and letting God direct your service so you don't end up overwhelmed?

11. What is some kind of service action, project, or ongoing ministry your small group could do together?

For prayer direction and additional resources for your group, you might want to review the final section of chapter 5 titled "Diving into Reckless Service" on page 107.

Session 6

Reckless Relationships

(DVD) **Watch:** "Session 6—Reckless Relationships" on the *Reckless Faith* DVD

1. Tell about a person who has helped you grow in your faith and deepen your love for Jesus. How has God used this person to help you walk more closely with the Savior?

2. Who is a person God has placed in your life that you have the privilege of helping grow in their faith? How are you walking alongside of this person and helping them know and love Jesus more?

Read: Hebrews 10:23–25 and Ephesians 4:14–16

3. Why is it important for Christians to be in community and close relationship with other believers? What do we miss out on if we are not in regular fellowship with other followers of Jesus?

4. What does it mean to speak the truth in love to each other? Give an example of a time someone did this with you and tell how this affected your life and faith.

5. Who are the people in your life who watch your back and have permission to point out a problem in your attitudes and actions when they see it? Why is it vital for us to have a few people in our life who love us enough to speak the hard truth to us?

Read: Matthew 9:9–13 and 11:19

6. What does Jesus teach and model for us when it comes to having friendships with people who have not yet embraced faith in God? If we were to follow the example of Jesus when it comes to the way we interact with non-Christians, how might this change our lives?

7. Tell about some of the ways you are growing and developing friendships and connections with those who are not yet followers of Jesus. How can you grow your commitment to building strong relationships with spiritually disconnected people?

8. What gets in the way of your making time to grow your relationships with people who are not Christians? What can you do to get past these roadblocks and develop deeper friendships with these people?

Read: The section titled "Bridging Your Worlds" from chapter 6

9. What are ways you are building bridges between your Christian friends and the people in your life who are not yet Christ followers?

10. What are some specific ways you can build stronger connections between your nonbelieving friends and the people you know who are followers of Jesus?

11. What can you do as a small group to build relational bridges between your church friends and your non-believing friends? Take time to plan a Matthew Party and see what God does.

For prayer direction and additional resources for your group, you might want to review the final section of chapter 6 titled "Diving into Reckless Relationships" on page 125.

Session 7

Reckless Prayers

Watch: "Session 7—Reckless Prayers" on the *Reckless Faith* DVD

1. Tell about a person in your life who has lifted up consistent and passionate prayer for you. How have you seen this person's prayers influence your life?

2. Tell about your own rhythm of prayer. When do you pray, how do you pray, and what sort of prayers are part of your regular conversation with God?

Read: Galatians 5:22–23

3. What is a specific fruit of the Spirit that you know needs to grow in your life right now, and how can your group members join you in praying for this fruit to blossom?

4. What is one fruit of the Spirit you need to begin praying for a person in your life that you care about, and how can your group members partner with you in this ministry of praying "Grow Your Fruit" for this person?

Read: 1 Samuel 3

5. Tell about a time that God spoke to you with clarity. How did you respond to the Good Shepherd speaking to you?

6. When God speaks to you in his still small voice and whispers direction for your life, how do you know and discern it is God speaking? How do you respond if you are not sure it is God's whisper to you?

Read: 2 Kings 6:8–17

7. How were the eyes of Elisha and his servant different and how did this impact their faith and boldness?

8. Tell about a time you got a glimpse (with your physical eyes or with spiritual eyes) of God's presence, glory, and power. How did this awareness strengthen your faith?

Read: The section titled "Let My Heart Feel What You Feel" from chapter 7

9. Why is this such a reckless and dangerous prayer?

10. When our heart begins to beat with the heart of God and we notice the pain and brokenness in our world, everything changes. What are some of the ways we might begin to take reckless steps of faith when our heart is broken by the needs in our community and world?

11. What is an act of compassion or ministry of mercy your small group could do in your community to reflect the loving heart of God?

Read: The introduction to this chapter and also the section titled "Your Will Be Done!"

12. Why is it so easy to pray "My will be done" types of prayers over and over again?

13. How will our prayer lives be transformed if we begin to pray, "Your will be done," and lift up the reckless prayers taught in this session?

For prayer direction and additional resources for your group, you might want to review the final section of chapter 7 titled "Diving into Reckless Prayers" on page 145.

Session 8

Reckless Words

Watch: "Session 8—Reckless Words" on the *Reckless Faith* DVD

1. We have people in our lives who are a good model of what it looks like to talk about faith in natural and healthy ways. Tell about a person you know who has been a great example of sharing their faith in Jesus and doing it with both gentleness and boldness. How does their example inspire and help you share your faith with others?

Read: Romans 10:14–15 and 1 Peter 3:13–16

2. What do these passages teach us about the importance and tone of our words when it comes to communicating the grace and message of Jesus?

3. What are some examples of ways people try to share their faith that are not gentle or respectful?

4. What are some examples of ways we can communicate the message and grace of Jesus and do it with bold recklessness but still be respectful and gentle?

Read: The section titled "Committed to Reckless Words! Really?" from chapter 8

5. Tell the story of how you became a follower of Jesus and the difference your relationship with Jesus has made in your life.

6. Tell a story about how God showed up in power and did something surprising in your life. How might sharing this story with a spiritually curious person help them take a step forward in their faith journey?

7. Tell about a time you were going through a difficult situation and the presence of God was with you in a very personal and tangible way. How might sharing this story with a spiritually curious person help them take a step forward in their faith journey?

8. If someone said to you, "I want to become a follower of Jesus. I am ready right now to receive him," what would you say and how would you help them along?

9. Tell about a person in your life who is not a follower of Jesus yet but is on the road toward faith in him. How is God using you to help and encourage this person? How can your group members pray and support you as you seek to love, serve, and share reckless words with this person?

Watch: "Closing to *Reckless Faith*" on the *Reckless Faith* DVD

10. Take a moment to write down two or three things you hope people will remember about you when your life on this earth is over.

    Share one of these with your group and tell them why this is important to you.

11. The most important legacy we will leave behind when our life is over is people. When God uses you to bring his love, grace, and the saving message of the gospel to another person, this has eternal consequences. As you come to the close of the *Reckless Faith* study, what is one way your life will be different and how might God use this reckless new outlook to impact someone for eternity?

For prayer direction and additional resources for your group, you might want to review the final section of chapter 8 titled "Diving into Reckless Words" on page 171.

reading guide

This entire book is based on biblical truths about God's desire to lead us on an adventure for faithful recklessness. The book is broken into eight chapters that follow the eight weeks of the all-church growth experience. I encourage you to read a chapter each week before the Sunday worship service that addresses this topic of *Reckless Faith*. Then, take time to read the Bible passages each day as a preparation for your Sunday worship service and weekly small group. By reading the book chapter and the Scripture texts, you will learn from God's Word and be ready to go deeper with your whole congregation and your small group.

Week 1

Read: *Reckless Faith*, Chapter 1 – **From Domesticated to Adventurous**

    Day 1- Luke 9
    Day 2- Exodus 2
    Day 3- Exodus 3
    Day 4- Luke 3

Day 5- 1 Kings 18
Day 6- Judges 6
Day 7- Luke 5

Week 2

Read: *Reckless Faith*, Chapter 2 – **An Invitation to Reckless Faith**
Day 1- Luke 8
Day 2- 1 Corinthians 3
Day 3- Matthew 16
Day 4- Acts 6-7
Day 5- Matthew 4
Day 6- 2 Corinthians 6 & 10
Day 7- 2 Corinthians 11-12

Week 3

Read: *Reckless Faith*, Chapter 3 – **Reckless Love**
Day 1- Mark 12
Day 2- Romans 5
Day 3- John 21
Day 4- Matthew 6
Day 5- Luke 14
Day 6- Acts 16
Day 7- Acts 22

Week 4

Read: *Reckless Faith*, Chapter 4 – **Reckless Generosity**
Day 1- 2 Corinthians 9
Day 2- Malachi 3

Day 3- 1 Timothy 6
Day 4- Philippians 4
Day 5- James 1
Day 6- Luke 19
Day 7- Proverbs 11

Week 5

Read: *Reckless Faith*, Chapter 5 – Reckless Service
Day 1- John 13
Day 2- Mark 10
Day 3- Philippians 2
Day 4- Matthew 25
Day 5- 1 Peter 4
Day 6- John 19
Day 7- John 20

Week 6

Read: *Reckless Faith*, Chapter 6 – Reckless Relationships
Day 1- Acts 2
Day 2- Hebrews 10
Day 3- Ephesians 4
Day 4- Matthew 9
Day 5- Romans 12
Day 6- 1 Corinthians 12
Day 7- Matthew 11

Week 7

Read: *Reckless Faith*, Chapter 7 – Reckless Prayers
Day 1- Psalm 23

Day 2- Galatians 5
Day 3- John 10
Day 4- 1 Samuel 3
Day 5- 2 Kings 6
Day 6- Isaiah 6
Day 7- Revelation 1

Week 8

Read: *Reckless Faith*, Chapter 8 – **Reckless Words**
    Day 1- Ephesians 6
    Day 2- Romans 10
    Day 3- Acts 1
    Day 4- 1 Corinthians 15
    Day 5- 1 Peter 3
    Day 6- Matthew 28
    Day 7- Acts 9 & 22

notes

Introduction

1. The movie *A Mighty Wind* is a lighthearted spoof of the folk music scene. This illustration is not an endorsement of the movie but a humorous look at how safety consciousness can spin out of control.

2. This is not an incrimination of modern technology in general or video games in particular. I love technology and all three of my sons played some video games while growing up (with clear boundaries and limitations). I am also not suggesting that we try to turn back the clock. I am just taking note of how the world has changed and why we need to help people take intentional steps toward adventure and responsible recklessness in our increasingly tame culture.

3. See C. S. Lewis, *The Lion, the Witch and the Wardrobe* (HarperCollins). The Pevensie children are learning about Aslan from the Beavers, and they explain that Aslan is not a tame lion, but he is good.

Chapter 1 From Domesticated to Adventurous

1. Lest any reader still think this to be cavalier, it is not an affirmation of dangerous behavior. I laid out the ground rules and talked with my son about how to make the jump in the safest manner. I also stayed to make sure he had help if anything went wrong. I made sure it could be safe and reckless at the same time.

2. A reckless spirit and a responsible life are not mutually exclusive. Though my three sons love adventure and are always up for a new challenge, they are also very responsible and safe. At the writing of this book, my sons have been driving for a combined total of twenty-four years. At present they have no accidents (that were their fault) and only one ticket between the three of them!

3. Matthew 6:33.

4. Luke 9:23.

5. Through this book you will get a clear picture of the difference between irresponsible recklessness that breaks the heart of God and true reckless faith that brings glory to Jesus.

6. John 10:4.

7. See Proverbs 11:14; 15:22; 24:6.

8. Galatians 5:22.

9. Exodus 2–3.

10. Luke 3:23.

Chapter 2 An Invitation to Reckless Faith

1. Ivan Pavlov was the Russian physiologist and Nobel Prize winner in physiology and medicine in 1904 who became famous for developing the idea of classical conditioning.

2. The parable of the sower has been preached on and written about a lot through the years. Sadly, we tend to focus almost exclusively on the various kinds of soil in the story and we often miss the beauty and message of the sower.

Chapter 3 Reckless Love

1. Ephesians 2:8–9.

2. John 15:13.

3. 1 John 4:10.

4. John 3:16.

5. John 19:30.

6. Acts 1:8.

7. Mark 12:30.

8. Mark 12:31.

9. Matthew 26:69–75; Mark 14:66–72; Luke 22:54–62; John 18:15–18, 25–27.

10. Matthew 26:74.

11. John 21:15–23.

12. Matthew 4:19.

13. 1 Timothy 6:10.

14. *Hyperbole* is an intentional exaggeration for the sake of making a point. Jesus uses hyperbole on a number of occasions. Another example is found in Matthew 5:28–30.

15. Matthew 26:33.

16. Author's paraphrase of Matthew 26:34.

17. Matthew 26:35.

18. John 21:16.

19. Mark 12:28–31.

20. These are Latin terms for "to infinity" and "to the point of nausea."

21. Matthew 6:33.

22. Here are three of my favorite books written by Ajith Fernando: *The NIV Application Commentary: Acts* (Zondervan)—it is one of the only commentaries

I have read that is actually a page-turner!; *Jesus Driven Ministry* (Crossway); and *The Call to Joy and Pain* (Crossway).

23. Jim Elliot, along with four other men, was killed by a group of tribal men in Ecuador in 1956. They were seeking to reach this tribe with the message and love of Jesus.

24. This wonderful little book is published by Zondervan and is a collection of prayers of martyrs through the ages.

25. All of these prayers listed in this chapter and the history behind them are found in the book, Duane W. H. Arnold, comp. and trans., *Prayers of the Martyrs* (Grand Rapids: Zondervan, 1991).

26. Revelation 19:6–8.

27. 1 Corinthians 12, Romans 12, and Ephesians 4 all paint a beautiful picture of the body of Christ.

28. 1 Corinthians 12:26.

29. Matthew 7:14–16 and Acts 20:29.

30. Marshall wrote a wonderful book titled *Well-Intentioned Dragons: Ministering to Problem People in the Church* (Bethany). It is a practical and helpful book for anyone dealing with the challenges of tough people in their local church.

31. 2 Corinthians 11:21–29.

32. Acts 16 and 22.

33. Acts 16:23.

34. Acts 22:25.

35. Acts 22:29.

Chapter 4 Reckless Generosity

1. This really happened, but Larry is not his real name.

2. Matthew 6:21.

3. James 1:17.

4. A tithe is the first 10 percent that we give to God and his work. An offering is additional giving toward needs and the work of God in this world. Until we give a tithe, we cannot give an offering.

5. We *prayed*, got *perspective*, and were *patient* and the conviction remained. After running this through our Responsible Recklessness Matrix, we were still confident it was the right thing to do. We had to be obedient . . . even if it felt and looked reckless!

6. If you go on YouTube and search "How to Catch a Monkey," you can see the whole thing.

7. 1 Timothy 6:10.

8. If you want to get some helpful statistics or sponsor a child in need, check out the websites for World Vision International or Compassion International.

9. Learn more about Clara's Bags of Hope: http://bagsofhope.blogspot.com/p/meet-bags.html.

10. Luke 10:25–37.

11. There is not space in this chapter to write about the best way to accomplish this feat, but there are some amazing Christian resources devoted to helping you get debt free so you can grow more generous. Check out Dave Ramsey's Financial

Peace University or Crown Financial Ministries. These are both excellent programs for overcoming the grip of debt.

12. Psalm 119:89.

13. This is a true story with no embellishment. My unwise choice endangered my grandmother. This lesson has never left me.

14. Luke 3:11.

15. The full book title is *When Helping Hurts: Alleviating Poverty Without Hurting the Poor . . . and Ourselves* by Steve Corbett and Brian Fikkert (Moody).

Chapter 5 Reckless Service

1. This video was developed in partnership with Daybreak Church in Hudsonville, MI, and a gifted artist, Mark Courtney. Learn more about Daybreak Church at www.daybreak.tv. To see a portion of the Lufutuko documentary, see joshharney.com.

2. Terry Woychowski, who at the writing of this book is the VP of Global Launches for General Motors, sponsored a Michigan Tech Senior Design Team to design and build a "Human Powered Hammer Mill" that will be manufactured and distributed in sub-Saharan Africa. One of the things that sparked this vision in Terry's heart was when he watched the documentary, *LUFUTUKO*.

3. The film *LUFUTUKO* won the "Vertigo Music and Sound Design Award" at the Grand Rapids film festival in 2007.

4. This documentary was developed for an organization called Freedom Fields U.S.A. For more information, see www.ffusa.org.

5. This medical ministry team has been serving in Guatemala and other areas of the world for many years, bringing excellent medical care and the love and message of Jesus.

6. Mark 10:45.

7. Philippians 2:10.

8. Matthew 26:15.

9. John 13:13–15.

10. Ephesians 5:25.

11. Promise Keepers is a movement for men that calls them to deeper faith and service in their homes and world, in the name of Jesus.

12. Sherry and I wrote a book titled *Organic Outreach for Families: Turning Your Home into a Lighthouse* (Zondervan). This book digs into many ways we can offer reckless service as we bring the grace of Jesus to our neighbors, family, and friends.

13. Colossians 3:17.

14. For some great community service ideas, check out the website www.shorelinechurch.org and go to ministries/outreach/community outreach.

15. Acts 1:8.

16. If you want to learn about sponsorship, check out the websites for World Vision International or Compassion International.

17. To learn more about Seismic Shifts, check out the book titled *Seismic Shifts: The Little Changes That Make a BIG Difference in Your Life* (Zondervan).

18. Matthew 19:29–30.

Chapter 6 Reckless Relationships

1. Matthew 6:24 and 1 Timothy 6:10.
2. As a child, I was afraid there were monsters living under my bed. It might have been because my parents read me the book *Where the Wild Things Are* before I went to bed.
3. Psalm 19:10.
4. God exists in community: Genesis 1:26; 3:22; 11:7; Isaiah 6:8.
5. Deuteronomy 6:4.
6. In many churches, the previous pastor feels the need to leave when a new pastor comes. In some cases, the church demands that this happen. In some denominations, this is policy. Though I realize there are times this might be necessary, I do feel extraordinarily blessed to have someone like Howie investing in my life and serving as a partner, side by side in ministry.
7. Matthew 22:34–40.
8. Genesis 1:26;, 3:22;, 11:7; Isaiah 6:8.
9. This is one of the three ecumenical creeds (along with the Apostles' Creed and the Nicene Creed) that are embraced by almost all Christian churches. It is attributed to Athanasius (AD 293–373). This is the longest of the creeds and focuses primarily on the Trinity and the two natures of Christ.
10. Romans 12:3–8; 1 Corinthians 12:12–26; Ephesians 4.
11. Hebrews 10:25.
12. This little book is a great gift for people who visit your church, for students going away from home to college for the first time, or for anyone who wants a balanced understanding of finding a church and becoming part of a local congregation.
13. Philippians 2:6–8.
14. Romans 5:8.
15. John 3:16.
16. Matthew 9:9–13.
17. Matthew 11:19.
18. Matthew 5:13–16.
19. To learn more about organic outreach and reaching people naturally with the gospel of Jesus, I've covered the topic in my three-book series on this topic: *Organic Outreach for Ordinary People*, *Organic Outreach for Churches*, and *Organic Outreach for Families* (Zondervan).
20. Matthew 9:9–13.
21. Ibid.
22. Romans 12:1–2.

Chapter 7 Reckless Prayers

1. Luke 22:42.
2. Matthew 6:9–14.
3. Galatians 5:22–23.
4. Daniel Iverson wrote this simple prayer in 1926.
5. If you want to learn more about how God speaks to his children, I would encourage you to read chapter 6 of *Seismic Shifts*, a book I wrote some years ago,

and also *The Power of a Whisper: Hearing God, Having the Guts to Respond* by Bill Hybels (Zondervan).

6. 1 Samuel 3:9.

7. Here are two more wonderful books that will help you grow in your ability to talk with God in conversational ways: *Listening for God: How an Ordinary Person Can Learn to Hear God Speak* by Marilyn Hontz (Tyndale) and *God's Prayer Book: The Power and Pleasure of Praying the Psalms* by Ben Patterson (SaltRiver).

8. 1 Kings 19:12.

9. In chapter 6 of *Seismic Shifts*, I look at how God uses many ways to speak to his children. Some of them can be neglected or even rejected, but God is the same yesterday, today, and forever (Heb. 13:8).

10. Matthew 28:20.

11. 2 Kings 6.

12. Daniel 6:16–24.

13. Isaiah 6:1–7.

14. Revelation 1:12–18.

15. If you are not familiar with the dynamic ministry of Youth for Christ, learn more at www.yfc.net.

16. For more information on World Vision see www.wvi.org.

17. For more information on Samaritan's Purse see www.samaritanspurse.org.

18. John 11:35.

19. There are so many passages that emphasize both God's heart for the broken and hurting as well as his call for us to feel and take action: Deuteronomy 10:18; Psalm 146:9; Isaiah 1:17; Jeremiah 22:3 are a few examples.

20. James 1:27 and Mark 1:40–41.

Chapter 8 Reckless Words

1. John 14:6.

2. Matthew 5:13 and Colossians 4:6.

3. These studies include the Interactions Series, the New Community Series, and many others.

4. Matthew 28:19–20.

5. For more information on Organic Outreach, read *Organic Outreach for Ordinary People*, *Organic Outreach for Churches*, and *Organic Outreach for Families*. Also, look for free training resources at www.organicoutreach.org.

6. 1 Peter 3:15.

7. D. James Kennedy's *Evangelism Explosion* (Tyndale), Bill Hybels and Mark Mittelberg's *Becoming a Contagious Christian* (Zondervan), and my Organic Outreach books all give great tools for learning to tell your conversion story.

8. I do not include this story as recommendation for churches to do casino nights. I am simply recounting what reached me. I do love when churches think outside the box and plan events that will reach people who are far from God and who would not come to normal church gatherings.

9. Acts 9:1–19; 22:3–16; 26:9–18.

10. *Organic Outreach for Ordinary People* has a chapter on telling our story (giving a testimony) and telling his story (the gospel).

11. I love the books *Becoming a Contagious Christian*; *The Complete Evangelism Guidebook* by Scott Dawson (Baker); and the little classic, *The Master Plan of Evangelism* by Robert Coleman (Revell).

12. You might want to start with Romans 3:23; 6:23; 10:9–10; 10:13; 8:1; and 12:1–2.

13. There are some wonderful resources to help you lead a Bible study with a person who is spiritually curious. A great starting point would be to read *Seeker Small Groups* by Garry Poole (Zondervan).

14. *The Case for Christ* by Lee Strobel (Zondervan) is an excellent resource. You also might want to do a keyword search for "Apologetics" on the Baker Publishing Group website. You will find a number of excellent resources you could study with a friend who is spiritually curious.

15. We use a book I wrote called *Seismic Shifts*, because it covers all the basics from Bible study, prayer, worship, relationships, giving, sharing faith, and much more.

16. 1 Peter 3:15.

Kevin G. Harney (MDiv, Fuller Seminary; DMin, Western Theological Seminary) is the senior pastor of Shoreline Community Church in Monterey, California. Harney is the author or coauthor of *The U-Turn Church*, *Organic Outreach for Ordinary People*, *Organic Outreach for Churches*, *Organic Outreach for Families*, *Leadership from the Inside Out*, *Seismic Shifts*, *Finding a Church You Can Love*, and more than seventy small-group guides (written in partnership with his wife, Sherry), as well as curriculum and numerous articles. He also does extensive teaching and speaking both nationally and internationally.

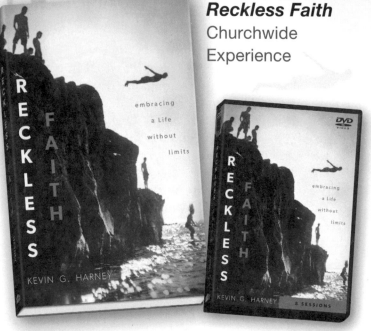

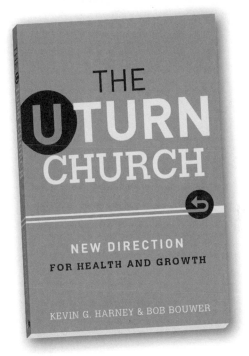